507.24 Gar
Gardner, Robert,
Science projects about
    the physics of toy$ 20.95
    games

W9-AJQ-763

Science Projects About the Physics of Toys and Games

Titles in the **Science Projects** *series*

Science Fair Projects—
Planning, Presenting, Succeeding
ISBN 0-89490-949-5

Science Projects
About Chemistry
ISBN 0-89490-531-7

Science Projects
About Electricity and Magnets
ISBN 0-89490-530-9

Science Projects About
the Environment
and Ecology
ISBN 0-89490-951-7

Science Projects
About the Human Body
ISBN 0-89490-443-4

Science Projects About
Kitchen Chemistry
ISBN 0-89490-953-3

Science Projects
About Light
ISBN 0-89490-529-5

Science Projects
About Math
ISBN 0-89490-950-9

Science Projects About
Methods of Measuring
ISBN 0-7660-1169-0

Science Projects About
Physics in the Home
ISBN 0-89490-948-7

Science Projects About the
Physics of Sports
ISBN 0-7660-1167-4

Science Projects About the
Physics of Toys and Games
ISBN 0-7660-1165-8

Science Projects
About Plants
ISBN 0-89490-952-5

Science Projects About the
Science Behind Magic
ISBN 0-7660-1164-X

Science Projects About Solids,
Liquids, and Gases
ISBN 0-7660-1168-2

Science Projects
About Sound
ISBN 0-7660-1166-6

Science Projects
About Temperature
and Heat
ISBN 0-89490-534-1

Science Projects
About Weather
ISBN 0-89490-533-3

Science Projects About
the Physics of
Toys and Games

Robert Gardner

Science Projects

Enslow Publishers, Inc.

40 Industrial Road	PO Box 38
Box 398	Aldershot
Berkeley Heights, NJ 07922	Hants GU12 6BP
USA	UK

http://www.enslow.com

Copyright © 2000 by Robert Gardner

All rights reserved.

No part of this book may be reproduced by any means
without the written permission of the publisher.

Library of Congress Cataloging-in-Publication Data

Gardner, Robert, 1929–
        Science projects about the physics of toys and games / Robert Gardner.
            p. cm. — (Science projects)
        Includes bibliographical references and index.
        Summary: Presents science projects and experiments exploring the physics of various
toys, including an air car, top, and balloon.
        ISBN 0-7660-1165-8
        1. Mechanics—Experiments Juvenile literature. 2. Toys—Experiments Juvenile
literature. 3. Science projects Juvenile literature. [1. Physics—Experiments. 2. Toys—
Experiments. 3. Experiments. 4. Science projects.] I. Title. II. Series: Gardner, Robert,
1929–   Science projects.
QC127.4.G38   2000
507'.8—dc21

                                                                99-42736
                                                                CIP

Printed in the United States of America

10 9 8 7 6 5 4 3

To Our Readers: We have done our best to make sure all Internet addresses in this book
were active and appropriate when we went to press. However, the author and the publisher
have no control over and assume no liability for the material available on those Internet sites
or on other Web sites they may link to. Any comments or suggestions can be sent by e-mail
to comments@enslow.com or to the address on the back cover.

Illustration Credits: Enslow Publishers, Inc., pp. 16, 19, 29, 37, 41, 46, 49, 51,
54, 57, 58, 60, 67, 69, 72, 73, 74, 79, 81, 82, 85, 88, 89, 90, 91, 94, 99, 101, 109,
119; Stephen F. Delisle, pp. 13, 20, 23, 25, 26, 28, 32, 107, 110, 113.

Cover Illustration: Jerry McCrea (foreground); © Corel Corporation (background).

Contents

Introduction **7**

1. *Toys You Can Make* **11**

    1-1* Make a Comeback Toy 12

    1-2* Make a Balancing Toy 15

    1-3* Make a Frictionless Toy Air Car 22

    1-4* Forces on Your Frictionless Toy Air Car 25

    1-5* Electric and Magnetic Forces on Your Frictionless
            Toy Air Car 27

    1-6* Make a Toy Electric Motor 31

    1-7* Make a Toy Telephone 34

    1-8* Make a Toy Spinning Top 36

2. *Science with Toy Cars and Trucks* **39**

    2-1* Toy Cars on Hills 40

    2-2* Marbles and Balls on Hills 43

    2-3* The Effect of Gravity on Hills 45

    2-4* Cars that Loop-the-Loop and Defy Gravity 48

    2-5* Cars, Hills, Brakes, and Gravity 51

    2-6* Magnetic Cars that Go Bump but Don't Touch 53

    2-7* Cars with "Springs" that Bump 56

    2-8* Ride Safely on a Toy Car 60

3. *Balloons, Balls, Bounces, and Spins* **63**

    3-1* Electrical Balloons: Getting Charged Up 64

    3-2* Balloons, a Ping-Pong Ball, and Bernoulli 66

    3-3* Balloons: Hot and Cold 68

    3-4   A Balloon in a Bottle 69

    3-5* Superball and Other Bouncers 71

    3-6* Throwing Curves with a Beach Ball 73

4. *Bring in the Artillery and Rockets* **77**

    4-1* The Speed and Range of Water Projectiles 78

*appropriate ideas for science fair project

4-2* Water "Bombs" Away! 84

4-3* Ascending Rockets: To What Height? 86

4-4* A Marble in Orbit 93

5. *Science with a Variety of Toys* **97**

5-1* Circling Wagons on the Move 98

5-2* Pulling Wagons 103

5-3 How Fast Does a Wind-Up Walking Toy Walk? . . . 106

5-4* How Does a Push-N-Go® Toy Work? 108

5-5* Why Does a Dipping Bird "Drink"? 110

5-6* Walking on Snow 112

5-7* Clay, Boats, and Aluminum Beverage Cans 115

5-8* How Thick Is a Soap Bubble? 117

5-9* Bubbles that Float 121

List of Suppliers **123**

Further Reading **125**

Index **127**

*appropriate ideas for science fair project

Introduction

We all enjoy playing with toys. So what could be a better way to learn about science than to experiment with toys? This book is filled with projects that use toys as the basis for experiments. By doing experiments that involve your favorite toys and games, you can learn a lot about science. By toys we mean not just the things that young children play with, but also party balloons, balls used in various sports, skis, sleds, toboggans, and a variety of other games and toys that adults enjoy, too.

Most of the materials you will need to carry out your investigations can be found in your home or in a toy store. Some of the specific toys used in Chapter 5 can often be bought at garage sales or in secondhand stores.

For some of the activities, you may need one or more people to help you. It would be best if you work with friends or adults who enjoy science as much as you do. In that way you will all enjoy what you are doing. **If any danger is involved in doing an experiment, it will be clearly stated in the text. In some cases, to avoid any danger to you, you will be asked to work with an adult. Please**

do so. We do not want you to take any chances that could lead to an injury.

Like a good scientist, you will find it useful to record your ideas, notes, data, and anything you can conclude from these projects in a notebook. Record keeping will allow you to keep track of the information you gather and the conclusions you reach. Using your notebook, you can refer to what you have done that may help you in doing other projects in the future.

Science Fairs

Most of the projects in this book will be appropriate for a science fair. Those projects are indicated with an asterisk (*). However, judges at such fairs do not reward projects or experiments that are simply copied from a book. For example, plugging numbers into a formula you do not understand will not impress judges. A graph of data collected from experiments you have done that is used to find a relationship between two variables would be more likely to receive serious consideration.

Science fair judges tend to reward creative thought and imagination. It is difficult to be creative or imaginative unless you are really interested in your project. Consequently, be sure to choose a subject that appeals to you. And before you jump into a project, consider, too, your own talents and the cost of materials you will need.

If you decide to use a project found in this book for a science fair, you should find ways to modify or extend it. This should not be difficult, because you will probably discover that as you do these projects new ideas for experiments will come to mind—experiments that could make excellent science fair projects, particularly because the ideas are your own and are interesting to you.

If you decide to enter a science fair and have never done so before, you should read some of the books listed in the Further Reading section, as well as *Science Fair Projects—Planning, Presenting, Succeeding*, which is one of the books in this series.

These books deal specifically with science fairs and will provide plenty of helpful hints and lots of useful information that will enable you to avoid the pitfalls that sometimes plague first-time entrants. You will learn how to prepare appealing reports that include charts and graphs, how to set up and display your work, how to present your project, and how to relate to judges and visitors.

Safety First

Most of the projects included in this book are perfectly safe. However, the following safety rules are well worth reading before you start any project.

1. Do any experiments or projects, whether from this book or of your own design, under the supervision of a science teacher or other knowledgeable adult.

2. Read all instructions carefully before proceeding with a project. If you have questions, check with your supervisor before going any further.

3. Maintain a serious attitude while conducting experiments. Fooling around can be dangerous to you and to others.

4. Wear approved safety goggles when you are working with a flame or doing anything that might cause injury to your eyes.

5. Do not eat or drink while experimenting.

6. Do not go on to a frozen lake or pond without permission from an adult.

7. Have a first-aid kit nearby while you are experimenting.

8. Do not put your fingers or any object other than properly designed electrical connectors into electrical outlets.

9. Never experiment with household electricity, except under the supervision of a knowledgeable adult.

10. Do not touch a lit high-wattage bulb. Lightbulbs produce light, but they also produce heat.

11. Many substances are poisonous. Do not taste them unless instructed to do so.

12. If a thermometer breaks, inform your adult supervisor. Do not touch either the mercury or the broken glass with your bare hands.

1

Toys You Can Make

In colonial America, most of the toys that children played with were homemade. Often, children made their own toys. In this chapter, you will see how to make some toys. The toys that you will make can be used to carry out a number of experiments that will help you to learn more about science. Perhaps by the time you finish this chapter you will want to make some toys of your own design. If you do, can you use any of them for experiments?

You can make a toy that will roll back to you after you give it a push that causes it to roll away from you along a smooth, level surface. To begin, use a hammer and a large nail to make two holes in the bottom of a 39-oz coffee can. The holes should be placed along the diameter of the bottom of the can. Each of the holes should be 1.9 cm (¾ in) from the center of the diameter, but on opposite sides of the center, as shown in Figure 1a.

Make a similar pair of holes in the can's plastic snap-on cover. You can make these holes by simply pushing the nail through the plastic. Next, use scissors to cut open a rubber band that is about 18 cm (7 in) long and 0.3 cm (⅛ in) wide. Thread the ends of the rubber band through the holes in the bottom and top of the can and tie the ends together over the top of the can, as shown in Figure 1b. Finally, have a friend hold the can and pull the plastic top away from the opening so that you can reach the rubber band inside the can. Be careful if the coffee can opening is sharp, because the metal can cut you. Use a twist-tie to fasten a weight, such as a fishing sinker or some heavy washers, to the center of both strands of the rubber band as shown. Be sure the weight is not touching the can but is suspended above the side of the can. Fasten the twist-tie securely to both strands of the rubber band. The weight will keep the center of the bands from turning.

Things you will need:

- hammer
- large nail
- empty 39-oz metal coffee can and plastic cover
- ruler
- marking pen
- scissors
- rubber band about 18 cm (7 in) long and 0.3 cm (⅛ in) wide
- a friend
- twist-tie
- a weight, such as a fishing sinker or heavy washers— about 60 g (2 oz) is good
- long, smooth, level surface

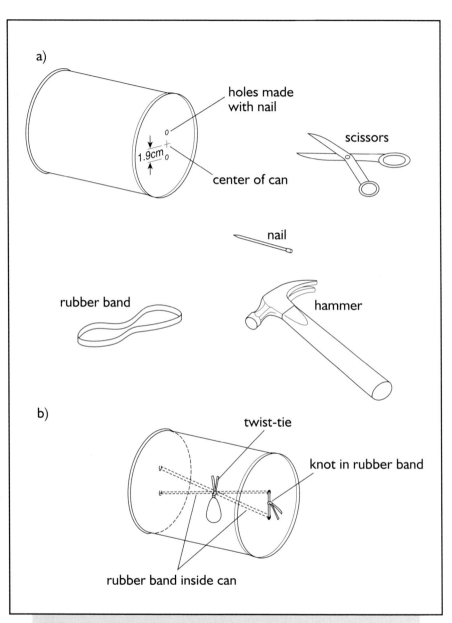

a)

holes made
with nail

scissors

center of can

1.9cm

nail

rubber band

hammer

b)

twist-tie

knot in rubber band

rubber band inside can

Figure 1. Use the materials shown in (a) to make the comeback toy shown in (b).

Replace the cover and place your homemade toy on its side on a smooth, level surface. Give it a push and watch it roll away from you. After a short time, it will stop and roll back to you. Can you explain why? If not, think about what is happening to the rubber band as the can rolls forward. What is happening to the weight?

Exploring on Your Own

You can do an experiment similar to Experiment 1-1 on a rope swing. Sit on the swing and have someone give you a push so that you swing around in one direction. What happens after you stop spinning in that direction? Can you explain why? How is your motion on the swing similar to the motion of the comeback toy? Are there any differences?

1-2*
Make a Balancing Toy

Obtain a wooden coffee stirrer or stick from a frozen fruit bar. Can you balance the stick on the tip of your finger?

You were probably able to balance the stick by laying it horizontally on your finger. But can you balance it vertically on your finger?

You can balance the stick vertically if you make a balancing toy. To make such a toy, wind the center portion of a 30-cm (12-in) length of 20-gauge copper wire tightly around the stick near one end, as shown in Figure 2. Bend the wire down on each side of the stick, make small hooklike bends at the ends of the wire, and place a heavy steel washer or nut on each hook.

You will find that the stick, even when vertical, will balance on your finger.

Things you will need:

- wooden coffee stirrers or Popsicle sticks
- 30-cm (12-in) length of 20-gauge copper wire
- 2 heavy steel washers or nuts
- full-length mirror
- an adult
- drill and small bit
- common pin
- a friend
- horizontal bar
- paper clips or short lengths of wire
- pen or pencil
- colored markers
- light cardboard
- glue
- drinking straw
- knife
- large potato

To understand why the stick will now balance in a vertical position, you need to know about its center of gravity. The center of gravity of any object is the point where all the weight of an object can be considered to be located. It is the object's balance point. When supported at its center of gravity, an object will not rotate in any direction unless pushed.

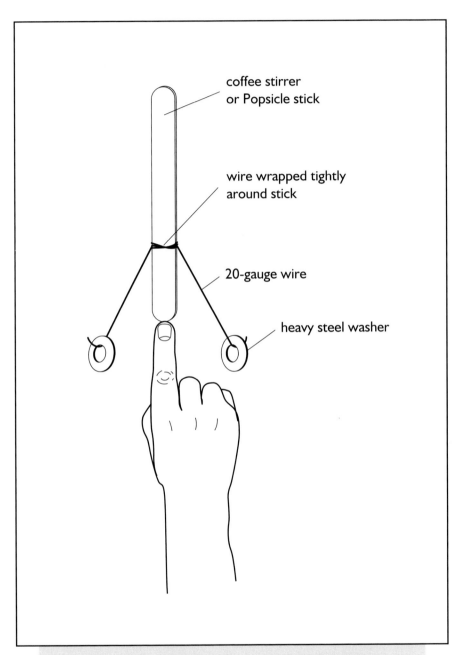

coffee stirrer
or Popsicle stick

wire wrapped tightly
around stick

20-gauge wire

heavy steel washer

Figure 2. A balancing toy is shown on the tip of an index finger.

As you found, the center of gravity of the stick alone is at its center. Before attaching the washers, when you placed the center of the stick horizontally on your finger, the stick balanced. But when you placed the stick vertically on your fingertip, it fell off. To see why, consider your own center of gravity. It is close to the middle of your body, several inches below your navel. Stand on one leg in front of a full-length mirror. Notice that to maintain your balance you must lean toward the leg on which you are standing. By so doing, you keep your center of gravity over the foot you are standing on. As a result, your body does not rotate about your center of gravity and cause you to fall. If you try to lift one leg without leaning, you will find that you begin to fall toward the leg you lifted.

Turn sideways in front of the mirror. Bend down and touch your toes as you watch your body in the mirror. You will see that as you bend you move your rump back. By so doing, you keep your center of gravity over your feet so that your body does not rotate and cause you to fall. If both your heels are against a wall, you will find that you cannot touch your toes. Why not?

Now, think about your balancing toy. You found it was impossible to balance the stick when it was vertical. You could not keep the stick's center of gravity directly over your fingertip. But when you added equal weights to opposite sides of the stick and kept them beneath the lower end of the stick, it was easy to make it balance. By adding weights, you lowered the center of gravity until it was below your fingertip.

You can do the same thing with the stick alone. Just put its center of gravity below its point of support.

Ask an adult to drill a small hole near one end of a stick like the one you used to make your balancing toy. Put a pin through the hole. Hold on to the head of the pin. Let the stick swing on the pin. Where does the stick come to rest? Where is its center of gravity relative to its point of support?

17

Ask a friend to hang from a horizontal bar with both hands. The bar should be slightly higher than your friend's reach so that his or her feet are off the floor. Then ask your friend to hang by one hand instead of two. Watch what happens to your friend's center of gravity. Is it below the hand from which he or she is suspended?

Move the wire that wraps around your balance toy farther up the stick so that the weights are above your fingertip, as shown in Figure 3a. Do you think the toy will balance now? Can you explain why?

What do you think will happen if you lower the weights again but bend the wire so that the weights are to one side of the stick, as shown in Figure 3b? Were you right? Can you explain the stick's new balance position?

Do you think you can make the stick balance if you substitute paper clips or short lengths of wire for the heavy washers or nuts? Try it. Were you right? Can you explain your results?

To amuse your friends or family, build the "always-upright clown." Draw a clown on a sheet of light cardboard. Add the proper colors and glue him to a drinking straw that you have stuck in the center of half a potato, as shown in Figure 4a. No matter which way you tilt the clown, he will always return to an upright position. Can you explain why? Using common materials you can find around your house, you might like to build some of the center of gravity toys shown in Figure 4b.

Exploring on Your Own

Design and build some more balancing toys.

Place the ends of a yardstick or meterstick on the index fingers of your outstretched hands. Slowly slide your hands together. At what point do they meet on the stick? Can you explain why they meet there? Now place a lump of clay near one end of the yardstick or meterstick and repeat the experiment. Where do your hands meet

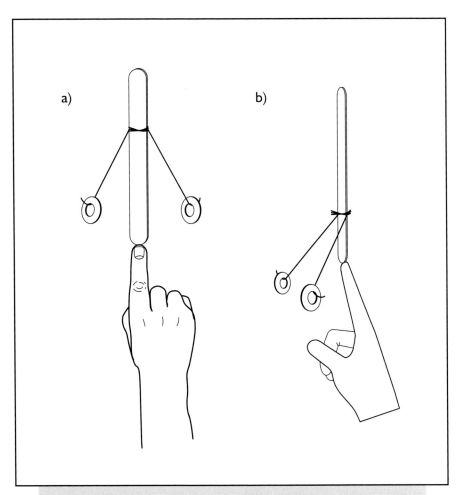

Figure 3. a) Will your balancing toy be stable if the weights are above your fingertip? b) Will the toy balance with both weights to one side and below your fingertip? If so, how will it look when balanced?

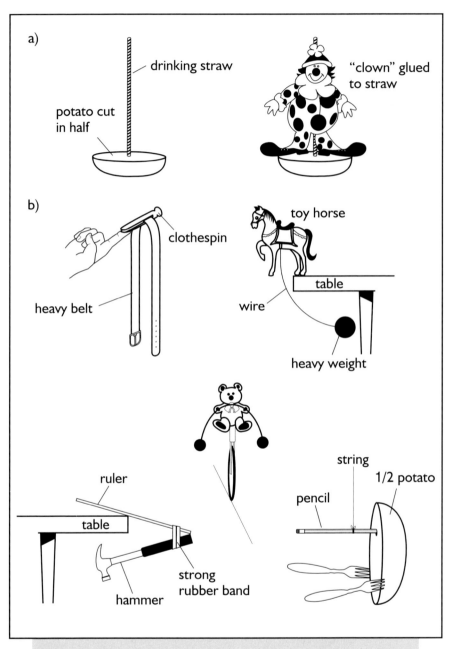

Figure 4. a) Make an always-upright clown. b) Some examples of balancing toys you might like to make.

this time? Can you offer an explanation? Design an experiment to test your explanation.

Investigate how the center of gravity is related to automobile safety.

Investigate how the center of gravity is related to sports. Of special interest might be the claim that a pole vaulter's center of gravity passes under, not over, the bar.

1-3*
Make a Frictionless Toy Air Car

You can build a frictionless toy air car from plywood, an empty thread spool, and a 12-inch balloon. **Ask an adult** to help you build the car. You will need a square piece of ¼-in plywood 7.5 cm (3 in) on a side. The plywood should be smooth on both sides. If the lower side of the wood square is not perfectly smooth, use some sandpaper to make it so.

Ask an adult to drill a hole 1.5 mm (¹⁄₁₆ in) in diameter through the exact center of the wood square. An empty thread spool can then be glued to the center of the square. Alternatively, you can bore a hole through a cork and glue it to the wood square. In either case, be sure the hole through the spool or cork is in line with the hole that was drilled through the wood square (see Figure 5).

Place the air car on a very smooth, level surface, such as a kitchen or laboratory counter. Blow up a balloon and attach it to the spool as shown in the drawing. Release the neck of the balloon so air can flow through the spool and the hole in the square. The air will lift the car slightly, providing a nearly frictionless surface on which the air car can move. Give the car a gentle push. It should move at what appears to be constant speed along the smooth, level surface. If it does not, you may need to sand the lower surface of the wood again; you may need a stronger balloon to force more air through the hole; or you may need to make the hole bigger by using a slightly larger drill bit than the one you used before.

Things you will need:

- ¼-in plywood
- empty thread spool, or cork, cork borer, and glue
- 12-in balloon
- saw
- ruler
- an adult
- drill and bit (¹⁄₁₆-in)
- sandpaper
- smooth, level surface
- thin pieces of wood or newspapers
- table that has a smooth surface, or a long, smooth board
- carpenter's level

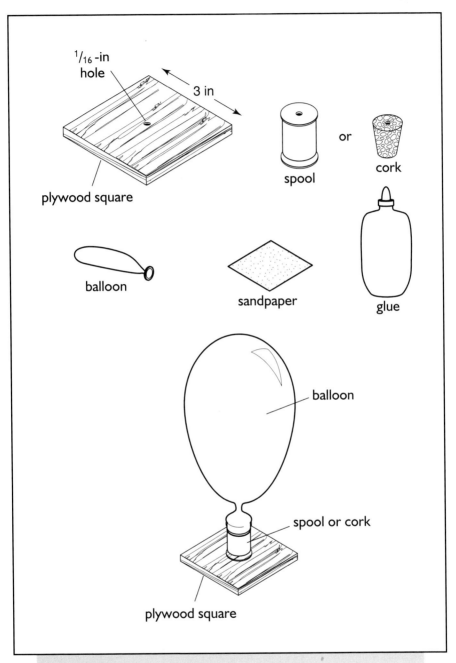

Figure 5. You can make an air car that is nearly frictionless.

What happens to the car when all the air has left the balloon?

Fill the balloon again and give the toy air car a push along a smooth, level surface. What do you notice about the car's speed if you give it a stronger push? A weaker push?

You know that if you drop your toy car or anything else, it will fall because the earth's gravity pulls everything toward its center. Similarly, a ball placed on even a slight incline will roll because the force of gravity pulls it closer to the earth.

Your air car is an excellent gravity detector. To see this for yourself, inflate the car's balloon and place the car on an incline. To make a slight incline, put thin pieces of wood or newspapers under two legs of a level table that has a smooth surface. You can do the same thing with a long, smooth board.

What happens when you place your air car at the top of the incline and let go? Why do you think the car moves faster and faster as it slides down the incline?

What happens to the way the car moves if you make the incline steeper? If you make it less steep?

How can you use your air car to tell whether a kitchen counter, a table, or a smooth floor is level?

Exploring on Your Own

Design and carry out experiments involving motion and colliding pucks on an air-hockey game.

As a thought experiment, suppose you were on board the space shuttle in orbit about the earth. Why would you not need a balloon to make the car move along a straight line along the shuttle at a constant speed?

As another thought experiment, what would happen if you placed your air car on a smooth, inclined board in the space shuttle? Would it move if you did not push it? How would it move if you did push it along the incline?

Forces on Your Frictionless Toy Air Car

You have seen that when gravity pulls your air car down an incline, the car moves faster and faster. Gravity is one way to exert a force (pull) on the car, but you can exert a force on the car yourself. You did that when you made the car move by giving it a push. You can also exert a force on the car by pulling it. If you attach a string to the top of the plywood with a piece of tape, you can pull it quite easily.

Things you will need:

- air car you made in previous experiment
- string
- tape
- smooth, level table
- washers
- paper clip

Fill the balloon of your air car and attach it to the spool or cork. Then use the string to pull the car over a smooth, level surface with

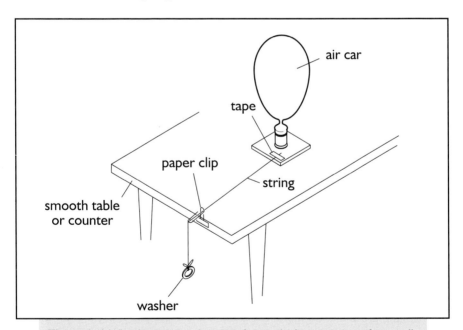

Figure 6. a) What happens to the air car's speed when a constant force pulls on it?

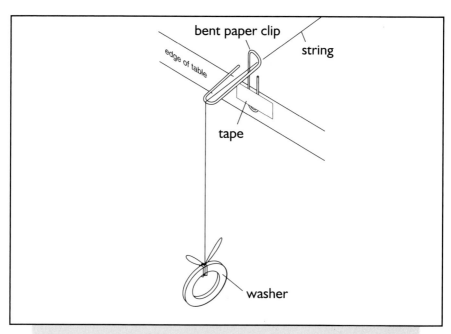

Figure 6. b) A close-up view of the free end of the string running through a bent paper clip.

a small but steady force, as shown in Figure 6a. What happens to the car's speed as you pull on it?

To apply a more constant force, attach the free end of the string to a washer, as shown in Figure 6b. Let the string, supported by a paper clip, hang over the end of a smooth table or counter on which the car will move. Describe the motion of the car when the washer pulls on it. What is causing the steady force on the air car now?

Attach a second washer to the string so that the pull (force) on the car is twice as great. How does the motion of the car with two washers pulling it compare with its motion when one washer pulls it? How do you think the motion of two air cars hooked together with tape and pulled by two washers would compare with the motion of one car pulled by one washer?

If you used a string to pull the car in the space shuttle, would its speed increase as you pulled it? Could you use a washer hanging over a table to pull your car in the space shuttle?

1-5*
Electric and Magnetic Forces on Your Frictionless Toy Air Car

Things you will need:

- air car you made in Experiment 1-3
- tape
- square- or disk-shaped ceramic magnets
- smooth, level table
- 2 balloons
- door frame
- string
- cloth
- plastic rulers, combs, or containers
- magnet
- long stick
- metal water pipe

Gravity and your muscles are not the only forces that can act on your air car. Magnets and electricity can push or pull it as well. Tape a small square- or disk-shaped ceramic magnet on to your air car, as shown in Figure 7.

Hold a second magnet close to the one on the air car. What happens? How can you tell that a force is acting? What happens to the direction of the force if you turn the magnet you are holding around?

If the two magnets are a fixed distance apart, the force will be constant. What happens to the speed of the air car when you use the magnets to exert a constant force? What happens to the strength of the magnetic force if you bring the two magnets closer together? How do you know?

How can the magnets be used as a brake to reduce the car's speed? If you keep the "brakes" on, can you make the car back up?

If you live in an area where winter brings cold weather, the air inside a building will be dry. In dry winter air, or on any day when the humidity is low, conditions are ideal for doing experiments with static electricity. *Static* means *stationary*. So static electricity involves electrical charges that are not moving.

Static charges leak away quickly in humid air, but in dry air you can charge many objects by simply rubbing them with a cloth or

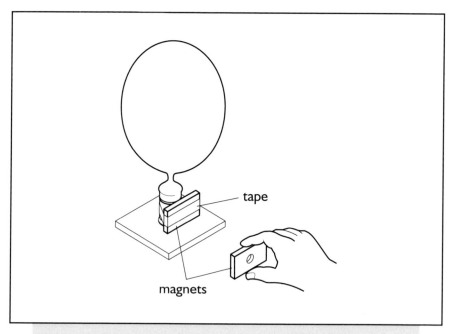

Figure 7. Can magnetism be used to move an air car?

paper. On such a day, blow up two identical balloons and seal them. Then hang the balloons from a door frame, using tape and strings, as shown in Figure 8. Charge both balloons by rubbing them with a cloth. Notice how the like-charged balloons repel each other. Try charging other objects such as plastic rulers, combs, and plastic containers. Do these objects all repel the balloons, or are the balloons attracted to some of them? Does the distance between charged objects have any effect on the strength of the force between them? How can you tell?

Objects that attract the balloons are said to carry a charge opposite that of the balloon. For example, if the balloons are positively charged, a charged object that attracts the balloons has a negative charge. After charging these objects, has any charge collected on your hands or clothes? How can you find out? Has a charge collected on the cloth?

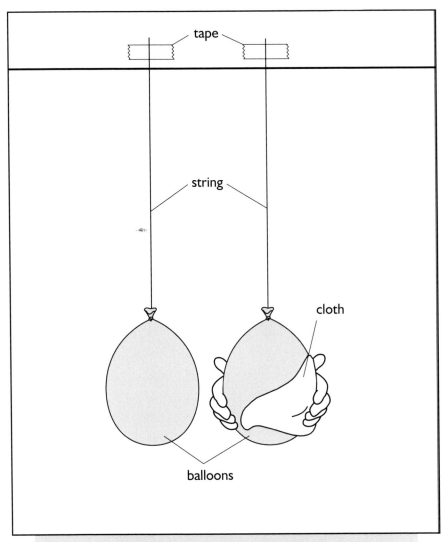

Figure 8. Suspend two balloons from strings. Charge the balloons by rubbing them with a cloth.

Tape a magnet to a long stick. Touch the magnet to a metal water pipe to remove any charge that may be on it. Then bring the magnet near, but not touching, a charged balloon. Does the magnet exert any force on the charged balloon? What does this tell you?

From what you have learned, use static electricity to exert a force on your air car. How can you use electric charge to accelerate your car? How can you use electric charge to act as a brake on your car?

Exploring on Your Own

Investigate the history of electricity and magnetism. Why did early scientists think magnets should exert forces on static charges? Is there a connection between electricity and magnetism? If there is, what is it?

The air car you made can operate for only a few seconds before its air must be replenished. Design and build a nearly frictionless car that can operate for minutes instead of seconds.

1-6*
Make a Toy Electric Motor

An electric motor is basically a coil of wire that turns in a magnetic field. To make a toy electric motor, you can begin by making the coil. Wrap a 30-cm (12-in) length of 24-gauge enamel-coated copper wire four times around the width of a ruler. Remove the coil of wire from the ruler. Wrap the two free ends of the wire once around opposite sides of the coil and extend them straight out from the coil (see Figure 9a). Use two small pieces of tape to hold the coiled wires in place. The entire length of the coil and extended wires should be about 3 inches. If the wires extending from the coil are too long, snip off part of their ends with a pair of wire cutters. Use sandpaper to remove the enamel from the two wires that extend out from the coil.

Things you will need:

- 30-cm (12-in) length of 24-gauge enamel-coated copper wire
- ruler
- tape
- wire cutters
- sandpaper
- two 10-cm (4-in) pieces of bare 20-gauge copper wire (or paper clips)
- thumbtacks
- short, soft pine board
- 2 flat, square or round ceramic or rubberized magnets
- insulated wires
- 2 D-cells and battery holder(s)

Next, make supports for the coil using bare 20-gauge copper wire (or paper clips) and thumbtacks, as shown in Figure 9b. Use thumbtacks to hold the supports upright on a small length of a soft pine board. Put the two bare ends of the wires extending from the coil through the loops of the supports. Place a magnet beneath the coil. Use insulated wires to connect two thumbtacks to a two-D-cell battery, as shown in Figure 9c. If a two-cell holder is not available, two one-cell battery holders can be connected with a wire. Give the coil a little flip with your fingers and watch your motor spin.

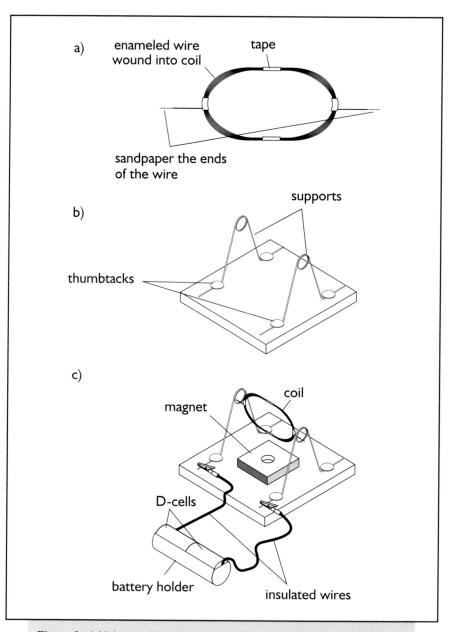

Figure 9. a) Make a coil by winding 30 cm of enameled wire around a ruler. Use sandpaper to remove the enamel from the ends of the wire. b) Make supports for the coil from two 10-cm (4-in) pieces of bare copper wire or paper clips. Use thumbtacks to hold the supports in place on a small, soft pine board. c) Connect two D-cells to the supports and give the coil a slight push to start it spinning.

Will the motor work if you use only one D-cell? What can you do to make the motor turn faster? What can you do to make the motor turn the other way? Can you use two magnets and make the motor turn? If so, where should you place the magnets?

Exploring on Your Own

If you made a diagram of your motor and showed it to an electrical engineer or physicist, he or she might tell you that your motor will not work because it has no commutator. What is a commutator? After you showed the doubting scientist or engineer that your motor does work, could you explain to him or her how and why it does work?

1-7*
Make a Toy Telephone

You can build your own private-line toy telephone. Use a small nail to make a hole in the bottom of each of two plastic-coated coffee cups. Then thread the ends of a long piece of monofilament fishing line through the holes. Tie the ends of the line to paper clips inside the cups. In that way the line will stay connected and can be made taut. Each cup

Things you will need:

- small nail
- 2 plastic-coated coffee cups
- monofilament fishing line
- paper clips
- a friend
- measuring tape
- garden hoses
- 2 large metal funnels

serves as both transmitter and receiver. Use your toy telephone to carry on a conversation with a friend who will speak into and listen through the other cup.

What is the maximum range of your telephone? What other materials can you use as "telephone lines"? Does the tautness of the line affect the transmission of sound? If so, how does it affect transmission? Does the frequency of the sound affect transmission—that is, are low frequency sounds, such as thunder, heard better than those with a high frequency, such as squeaks?

You can also make a toy telephone system by joining two or more garden hoses. As you speak softly into one end of the hose, have a friend listen with his or her ear against the other end. When your friend speaks into the other end of the hose, can you hear him or her?

Is the transmission of sound improved if you put a funnel into the end of the hose into which you speak? Is sound transmission improved if you put a funnel into the end of the hose where you listen? Is the transmission of the sounds affected by their frequencies? If so, how is it affected?

How could you arrange the hoses so that they could become an intercom system for your home?

Exploring on Your Own

Carry out an investigation to find out how a real telephone works.

How do dolphins and other water mammals use echolocation to locate objects? Is there any evidence to indicate that these mammals communicate with one another?

1-8*
Make a Toy Spinning Top

Newton's first law of motion tells us that a moving object will continue moving with a constant velocity unless a force acts on it. In much the same way, a spinning top will keep on spinning unless a force is applied to it.

You can make a toy top of your own from a pencil and some disks made of thin cardboard. To begin, sharpen the pencil, but do not make it too sharp. The end of the pencil lead should be about a millimeter in diameter. Use wire cutters to cut off the pencil so that it is about 6 cm (2.5 in) long.

Things you will need:
- pencil
- thin cardboard
- pencil sharpener
- ruler
- wire cutters
- drawing compass
- scissors
- smooth, level surface, such as a tabletop
- a friend
- stopwatch or a watch or clock with a second hand or mode
- pencil or pen
- notebook

Use a drawing compass to make circles about 8 cm (3 in) in diameter on thin cardboard, as shown in Figure 10a. Cut out the circular cardboard disks with scissors and mark their exact centers with a pencil.

On a smooth, level surface, try to make the pencil spin by itself. Next, make a more conventional toy top by pushing the pencil point straight through the center of one of the disks. The point of the pencil should extend about 2 cm (¾ in) below the bottom of the disk (see Figure 10b). Set this top spinning on the smooth surface. Ask a friend to use a stopwatch or a watch or clock with a second hand or mode to measure the time the disk keeps spinning before its edge hits the surface. Do this ten times and determine the average length of time the top spins.

Do you think the mass of the disk has any effect on the time that the top spins? To find out, add a second cardboard disk to the

36

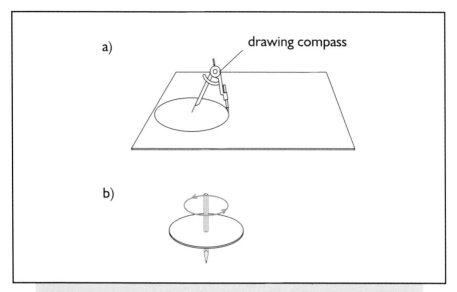

a)

drawing compass

b)

Figure 10. a) Use a drawing compass to mark circles on a piece of thin cardboard. b) Make a toy top from the disks and a short length of pencil.

top. Again, measure the spin time for ten spins and calculate the average spin time.

What do you think will happen to the spin time if you add a third disk to your top? Try it! Were you right?

Exploring on Your Own

Does the position of the mass affect the top's spin time? Will a disk with most of its mass farther from the pencil's shaft spin longer than one with the mass close to the pencil? Design and carry out an experiment to find out.

Investigate the laws of conservation of momentum and conservation of angular momentum. How are these laws related to a spinning top?

2

Science with Toy Cars and Trucks

The next time you go to a toy store, look at the great variety of toy cars and trucks that you can find on the shelves. In this chapter, you will see how some of these toy vehicles can be used in a variety of science experiments. The experiments will involve the effect of gravity on cars, friction, brakes, making cars do loop-the-loops, collisions, safety belts, and lots more. You will be doing a lot of experimenting. Keep a notebook handy to record your results.

2-1*
Toy Cars on Hills

After riding your bicycle up a long hill, it feels good to reach the top and coast down the other side. In this experiment, you will use toy cars and a length of track to investigate how the height and length of the hill affect the distance a car will coast.

Place one end of a length of track 60 to 90 cm (2 to 3 ft) on a block or book, as shown in Figure 11. The lower end of the track should rest on a long, smooth, level surface so that a toy car can travel as far as it will go after rolling down the "hill" made by the track.

Start a toy car from the very top of the track. Let it roll down the hill and along the level surface until it stops. Use a meterstick, yardstick, or tape measure to find out how far the car traveled after it reached the bottom of the ramp. Repeat the experiment four or five times and record the average distance.

Things you will need:

- track 60 to 90 cm (2 to 3 ft) long (Darda®, Hot Wheels®, and Majorette® make tracks, or you can make your own from cardboard and fold up the sides so the car will not fall off)

- long, smooth, level surface

- several Hot Wheels®, Matchbox®, or similar small toy cars

- 3 identical toy blocks or books

- meterstick, yardstick, or tape measure

- pen or pencil

- notebook

- balance or scale

- clay

- shorter or longer piece of track

Now try another car and measure the average distance it travels over four or five runs. Does it go the same distance as the first car, farther, or not as far?

Predict what will happen to the distance a car travels if you place the end of the track on two blocks or books instead of one. Then make several runs with one of the toy cars. Were you right? Did the car travel twice as far? The same distance? Not as far?

40

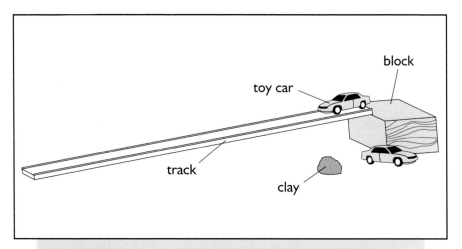

Figure 11. How far will the car go after it rolls down the incline?

Predict the distance a car will travel when you place the end of the ramp on three blocks or books. Test your prediction. Were you right? Record the results of these experiments.

Weight and Distance

Do you think the weight of a car will affect the distance it travels after rolling down the hill? To find out, weigh one of the cars on a balance or scale. Then prepare a lump of clay that has the same weight.

Let the car roll down the track several times and find the average distance it travels. Then hold the car in one hand so that no pressure is applied to the wheels as you gently press the lump of clay onto the top of the car with your other hand. You have now doubled the car's weight. Does the added weight affect the distance the car travels after rolling down the ramp? If it does, how does it affect it?

Length of Incline and Distance

Do you think the length of the ramp will affect the distance the car travels after rolling down the hill? To find out, measure the average distance the car travels beyond the ramp you have been using. Then test the same car several times on a ramp that is shorter or longer. Does the length of the ramp affect the distance the car travels after it reaches the end of the track? Can you explain why? Design and carry out an experiment to test your explanation.

Exploring on Your Own

Do real cars on hills behave in the same way that the toy cars did in this experiment? Design experiments to find out. Then, **ask an adult** to drive a car while you carry out your experiments.

2-2*
Marbles and Balls on Hills

In the previous experiment, you found out how far toy cars travel after rolling down an incline. You can use much of the equipment you used in that experiment to investigate how far different spheres will travel after rolling down an incline.

Place one end of a length of track 60 to 90 cm (2 to 3 ft) on a block or book. The lower end of the track should rest on a long, smooth, level surface so that a marble will travel as far as it will go after rolling down the track.

Start a marble from the very top of the track. Let it roll down the hill and along the level sur-

Things you will need:

- track 60 to 90 cm (2 to 3 ft) long (Darda®, Hot Wheels®, and Majorette® make tracks, or you can make your own from cardboard and fold up the sides so the marble will not fall off)

- long, smooth, level surface

- 3 identical blocks or books

- meterstick, yardstick, or tape measure

- pen or pencil

- notebook

- marbles of the same and different diameters

- balls: tennis, baseball, golf, croquet, Ping-Pong, rubber, etc.

face until it stops. Use a meterstick, yardstick, or tape measure to find out how far it traveled after it reached the bottom of the ramp. Repeat the experiment four or five times and record the average distance.

Now try another marble of the same diameter and measure the distance it travels over four or five runs. Does it go the same distance as the first one, farther, or not as far?

Predict what will happen to the distance the marble travels after rolling down a track when the end of the track is on two blocks or books instead of one. Then try it several times. Were you right?

Predict the distance the marble will travel when you place the end of the ramp on three blocks or books. Test your prediction. Were you right?

Do you think the marble's weight will affect the distance it travels after rolling down the hill? To find out, repeat the experiment with a larger marble. What do you find? Does the weight of the marble affect the distance it travels? If it does, how do you know it was not caused by the size rather than the weight of the marble? Design and carry out an experiment to find out.

Now try some other spheres. Which do you think will roll farther after leaving the ramp, a baseball or a marble? How about a golf ball? A Ping-Pong ball? A tennis ball? A croquet ball? Other balls? Of all the spheres you tested, which one traveled the farthest after leaving the ramp? Can you explain why it traveled farther than the others?

2-3*
The Effect of Gravity on Hills

Hang a large toy truck from a spring scale or a long rubber band. Although the rubber band cannot measure weight, measuring the length of the rubber band will allow you to compare weights.

Things you will need:

• large toy truck

• spring scale or long rubber band

• smooth board about 1 m (3 ft) long

• blocks or books

• ruler

Place blocks under one end of a smooth board about 1 m (3 ft) long. The raised end of the incline should be about 30 cm (1 ft) above the floor (see Figure 12).

Place the truck at the top of the inclined board. Use a spring scale or rubber band to measure (or compare) the force with which gravity pulls the truck down the incline. Record your results. Is the force more, less, or the same as the truck's weight that you measured before?

Now use more blocks to raise the end of the board so it is about 60 cm (2 ft) high. Again, use the spring scale or rubber band to measure (or compare) the force with which gravity pulls the truck down the incline. Is the force more or less than it was when the board was less steep? What will the force be when the incline is at an angle of 90°—that is, when it is vertical? Measure (or compare) the force. Were you right?

Again, place the board so that one end of the incline is 30 cm (1 ft) higher than the end on the floor. How much force is needed to pull the truck along the incline? How much force is needed to lift the truck straight up from the floor to the top of the incline?

Does an inclined plane make it easier to move an object upward? Why?

Turn the truck upside down so that its top rather than its wheels are on the incline. What force is required to drag the truck up the

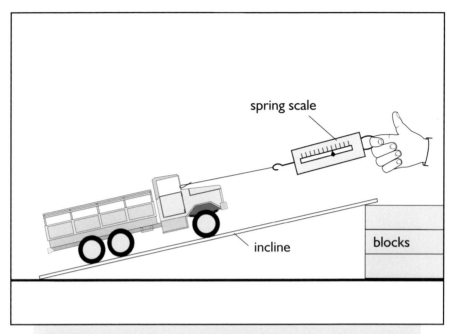

Figure 12. How does the force of gravity along the incline compare with the weight of the truck when it is pulled vertically by gravity?

incline now? How does the force needed to pull the upside-down truck up the incline compare with the force needed to pull the truck on wheels up the incline? How can you account for the difference in the force needed to move the truck under these different conditions?

Exploring on Your Own

If you slide down a snowy hill on a sled, does the weight on the sled affect the distance it travels after reaching the bottom of the hill?

The force needed to roll an object up an incline is less than the force needed to lift it straight up to the same height. But do you do less work when you roll an object up an incline than you do when you lift it? To answer this question, you need to first investigate how work is defined in science. Then you can measure work under the different conditions.

Why do you think engineers define the screw as an inclined plane? Find two screws that have the same diameter but a different number of threads per centimeter or inch. Which screw do you think will be easier to turn with a screwdriver? Why?

Make a list of the places where you see inclined planes being used. Try to explain why they are used at each site you observe.

2-4*
Cars that Loop-the-Loop and Defy Gravity

Construct a loop-the-loop to which you can attach a straight length of track. It should be possible to raise the end of the straight track well above the highest point of the loop (see Figure 13).

As you may know, an object that is raised to a height above the ground or floor has gravitational potential energy. It can do work if it falls back to the floor. If a ball rolls down an incline shaped like a roller coaster track, the potential energy is converted to kinetic energy (the energy associated with motion). Theoretically, the ball should reach the same height from which it started if it rolls up a similar incline after reaching the bottom of the incline it rolled down. Of course, it never does because it loses some energy due to friction between the ball and the incline on which it rolls.

If you let a toy car roll down an incline like the one shown in Figure 13, at what height (h) must you release the car before it can successfully complete the loop-the-loop? Is the release height required for the car to complete the loop-the-loop the same for all cars? If not, what might cause any differences in the required release height?

Repeat the experiment using a variety of spheres, such as marbles and small balls—rubber, golf, and Ping-Pong. From what height does each sphere have to be released in order to make it around the loop? Do the various spheres differ in the height from which they must be released in order to make it around the loop? If they do, can you explain why?

Things you will need:

- loop-the-loop track (from Darda®, Hot Wheels®, or other source)
- toy cars such as Lego®, Hot Wheels®, Matchbox®, etc.
- rulers, meterstick, or yardstick
- spheres such as marbles, and small balls—rubber, golf, and Ping-Pong
- calculator that can find square roots
- electric toy car

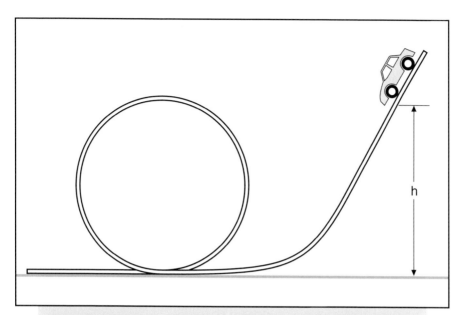

Figure 13. Small toy cars and balls can roll down the track and do a loop-the-loop. What is the minimum height, *h*, required for a car or ball to make it around the loop-the-loop?

It can be shown that theoretically there is a minimum height from which an object must be released to complete the loop. That theoretical height, as measured from the top of the loop, is ¼ the diameter of the loop.

Measure the diameter of the loop-the-loop and then add ¼ of that diameter. The sum of those two numbers should give you the minimum theoretical height from which an object must be released to make it around the loop. By how much did each of the cars and spheres you tested exceed the theoretical minimum height?

Electric Cars on the Loop

Many Darda®, Hot Wheels®, and other loop-the-loop tracks include a small toy car with a rechargeable motor. After charging the motor, the car will follow a track that includes one or more loop-the-loops.

The directions that come with the toy may tell you to charge the car's electric motor for a specific length of time, such as 10 seconds.

Usually, the specified time will charge the motor enough to make it go around the track several times.

For how long must you charge the car's motor so that it will go around a single loop-the-loop just once?

As you can see, the car with a minimally charged motor moves slower than one that is fully charged. But how fast does it move? What is the approximate minimum speed for a car to make it around the loop-the-loop?

Theoretically, the minimum speed required for the car to make it around the loop is approximately the square root of 5 m/s² times the diameter (D) of the loop, that is:

V = minimum velocity; m/s = minimum speed in meters per second;
D = diameter of the loop.

$$V(minimum) = \sqrt{(5 \text{ m/s}^2 \times D)}.$$

For example, if the loop has a diameter of 0.3 m (30 cm), the theoretical minimum speed required for the car to make it around the loop is

$$\sqrt{5 \text{ m/s}^2 \times 0.3 \text{ m}} = 1.2 \text{ m/s}.$$

Design your own experiment to measure the minimum speed required for the car to make it around the loop. How does the speed you measure compare with the theoretical minimum speed?

Exploring on Your Own

Work out why the minimum height for an object to complete the loop-the-loop as measured from the bottom of the loop is 1.25 times the diameter of the loop.

Work out why the minimum speed for a car to make it around a loop-the-loop is approximately the square root of 5 m/s² x the diameter of the loop.

2-5*
Cars, Hills, Brakes, and Gravity

Find a good-size toy car or truck with wheels that turn freely. Place the toy car or truck at one end of a long, smooth board. Slowly lift one end of the board until the vehicle starts to roll. What is the slope of the incline

Things you will need:

- good-size toy car or truck (10 cm [4 in] or more in length) with wheels that turn freely

- long, wide, smooth board

- rubber bands

when it starts to roll? (See Figure 14.) What does this tell you about the friction between the truck wheels and the board?

In the early 1900s, when cars were just beginning to replace horses, some of the cars had brakes on only one pair of wheels. Do you think the brakes were on the front or rear wheels? After you carry out this experiment, you should be able to answer this question.

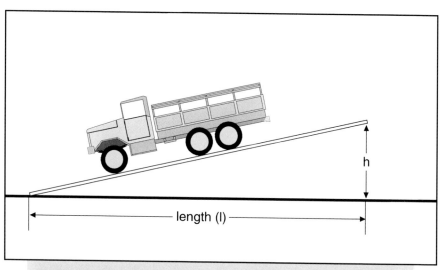

Figure 14. The slope of an incline is the height, h, to which one end is raised divided by the length shown, l. If h is 5 cm and l is 50 cm, the slope is $5 \div 50 = 0.1$ (1/10).

Place the toy vehicle on the board again. Lift the board a little and the truck will roll straight down. Wrap a rubber band around both the front and rear wheels so that none of the wheels can turn. Will the car roll down the hill now? Will it slide down the hill if you make the hill steeper? How does the friction between the board and locked wheels compare to the friction between the board and wheels that are free to turn? How do you know?

Now, use a rubber band to prevent only the rear wheels of the car from turning. Leave the front wheels free to turn. Again, raise one end of the board until the car starts to slide. What happens to the car as it slides down the hill? Repeat the experiment, but this time use the rubber band on the front wheels only, leaving the rear wheels free to turn. What happens when the car slides this time? Do you think the front or the rear brakes on a car lock first when a driver steps on the brake pedal? On old cars that had brakes on only one pair of wheels, which pair, front or rear, had brakes?

Exploring on Your Own

Explain why the brakes on the front wheels of cars are made to take hold before the rear wheels.

2-6*

Magnetic Cars that Go Bump but Don't Touch

Find two small identical toy cars that have wheels with little friction. Use tape or rubber bands to fasten a rubberized or ceramic magnet to the front or rear of each car. Before you fasten a magnet to the second car, be sure the magnet is turned so that it will repel the magnet on the first car. Use a balance to weigh the cars. Their weights should be very nearly the same. If they are not, add a little clay to the lighter car until their weights are equal.

Place the two cars on a long, level piece of plastic track so that the magnets will repel as the cars approach one another, as shown in Figure 15. With one car at rest in the middle of the track, place the other car near the end of the track and give it a push so that it approaches the car at rest. What happens as the moving car approaches the car at rest? Repeat the experiment several times and closely observe what happens. What happens to the car that was at rest? What happens to the car that was in motion?

Switch cars (moving and stationary) and repeat the experiment. Are the results the same?

Next, prepare a piece of clay that has the same weight as one car. Hold the car in one hand so that no pressure is applied to the wheels as you gently press the lump of clay onto the top of the car with your other hand. Let the car that now weighs twice as much as the other serve as the stationary car and repeat the experiment. How do the cars behave this time? What is different about the way they interact now?

Things you will need:

- 2 identical toy cars—Lego®, Hot Wheels®, Matchbox®, or similar toy cars

- tape or rubber bands

- 4 or more rubberized or ceramic square or disk magnets (can be purchased at a Radio Shack store)

- 90-cm (3-ft) or longer piece of straight plastic track, such as those made by Darda®, Hot Wheels®, or Majorette®

- balance

- clay

- ruler

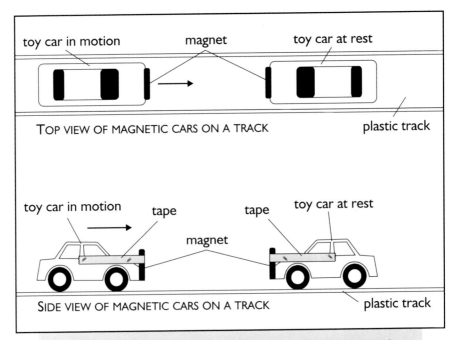

Figure 15. What happens as one magnetic car approaches the other?

Repeat the experiment, but this time have the lighter car at rest and put the heavier car in motion. What happens this time? How does this interaction differ from the previous one?

Hold another magnet with your fingertips. How can you use the magnet to make one of the magnetic cars move away from you? How can you use the magnet to make the car come toward you?

Place a ruler beside the magnet on one of the cars. Then, with your hand, move a single magnet toward the car so that the car is repelled by the magnet in your hand. At what distance between the two magnets does the car just begin to move? Repeat the experiment several times to be sure your results are consistent. Next, repeat the experiment with a stack of two magnets in your hand. At what distance between the magnets does the car start to move now? Try the experiment again with a stack of three magnets in your hand. Does the number of individual magnets in a stack of magnets affect the strength of the magnet as a whole? How do you know?

Exploring on Your Own

Early in the nineteenth century, scientists thought that electricity and magnetism were independent phenomena, even though both exhibited forces of attraction and repulsion. How did experiments performed by Hans Christian Oersted and Michael Faraday show that electricity and magnetism are related? You might begin your research in a science encyclopedia, and go on to books about electricity and magnetism.

Under adult supervision, carry out some of the experiments performed by Oersted and Faraday that show how electricity and magnetism are related.

2-7*
Cars with "Springs" that Bump

The previous experiment can be done in a different way without magnets. You will need two similar large toy trucks that have wheels with very little friction and two hacksaw blades. Use duct tape to fasten a hacksaw blade to the front of each truck, as shown in Figure 16. Be sure the two hacksaw blades are level and at the same height so that they will meet and bend as the trucks collide.

Things you will need:
- 2 large (more than 20 cm [8 in] long) toy trucks that have wheels with very little friction
- 2 hacksaw blades
- duct tape
- smooth level surface
- weights, such as stones, small bags of sand or pebbles, or similar items that can be used to add weight to the trucks
- balance to weigh trucks
- chair or some other heavy stationary object

With one truck at rest on a smooth level surface, give the other truck a push so that the springlike hacksaw blades (not the trucks) meet and bend. If the trucks turn sideways when they collide, you will have to add some weight to each truck. You could add stones, small bags of sand or pebbles, or whatever you can improvise. Be sure both trucks have the same weight.

When you are sure the trucks will not turn sideways as they collide, you are ready to begin the experiment. Place the two trucks about 30 cm (1 ft) apart on a long, level surface where the hacksaw blades can meet. With one truck at rest, give the other truck a push so that it approaches the car at rest. What happens as the hacksaw blades collide? Repeat the experiment several times and observe what happens closely. What happens to the car that was at rest? What happens to the car that was in motion?

Switch cars (moving and stationary) and repeat the experiment. Are the results the same?

Next, add weight to one truck so it is approximately twice as heavy as the other. Let the heavier truck be the stationary one as

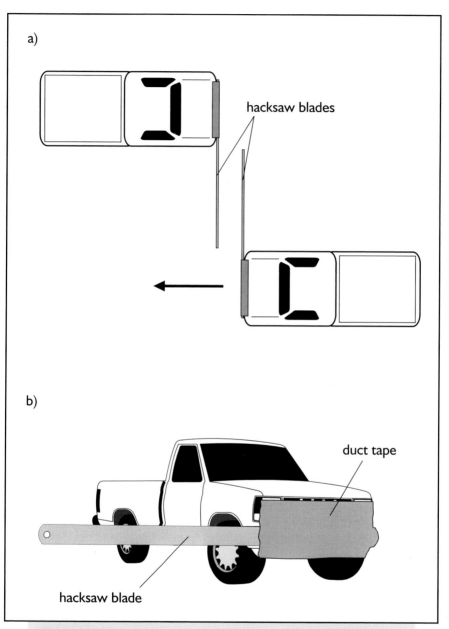

a)

hacksaw blades

b)

duct tape

hacksaw blade

Figure 16. a) A top view of toy trucks with attached hacksaw blades just before they collide. b) A view of the toy truck to show how the hacksaw blade is attached.

you repeat the experiment. How do the trucks behave this time? What is different about the way they interact now?

Repeat the experiment with the lighter truck at rest. What happens this time? How does this interaction differ from the previous one (Experiment 2-6)? How are they similar?

Disappearing Energy?

Watch closely as the hacksaw blades attached to the two trucks of equal weight collide. The moving truck has kinetic energy (energy of motion) as it approaches the stationary truck. After the moving truck loses its energy and comes to rest, the truck that was stationary moves away with most of the kinetic energy. But during the time they are interacting, some kinetic energy is lost. Is the energy really lost, or is it changed to some other form of energy?

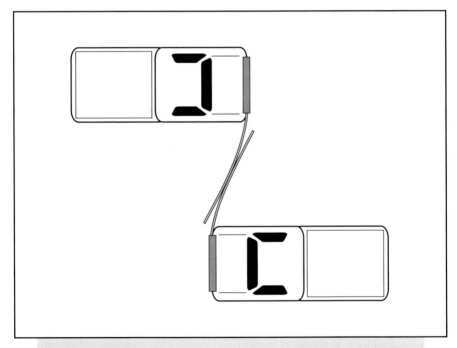

Figure 17. Top view of two toy trucks pushed together so that the hacksaw blades are bent. What happens when the trucks are released?

Possibly the lost kinetic energy is stored in the bent, springy hacksaw blades. You can carry out a simple experiment to find out. Push the two trucks close together so as to bend the hacksaw blades, as shown in Figure 17. This is what happens to the blades when the trucks interact. Now, suddenly release the trucks at the same time. What happens? Is there any evidence of kinetic energy when you release the trucks?

There is another way to see this change of kinetic energy to potential energy back to kinetic energy. Push one of the trucks so that its hacksaw blade hits a fixed object such as the leg of a chair on which someone is sitting. What happens? Does the truck, at some point during the collision, lose all of its kinetic energy? How do you know? Does it regain much of its kinetic energy after the collision? What is different about its motion after the collision as compared to its motion before the collision?

Exploring on Your Own

What is the law of conservation of energy? What evidence is there to support the law?

2-8*
Ride Safely on a Toy Car

In most states the law requires that you wear a seat belt when you ride in a car. This experiment will help you to understand why seat belts help to reduce traffic fatalities.

A doll can be used to represent an automobile passenger. Rest one end of a thin, wide board on some books or wooden blocks to make an incline. Place a toy car or truck or roller skate at the top of the incline and let it roll down the "hill" and onto a smooth level surface.

Things you will need:

- small doll
- strong, wide rubber bands
- large toy car or truck or roller skate
- wide board
- two concrete blocks
- smooth, level surface, such as a driveway, sidewalk, or concrete floor

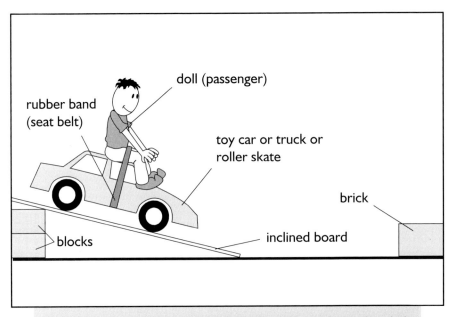

Figure 18. In this experiment, the "passenger" is firmly attached to the vehicle with a rubber band that acts like a seat belt.

Place a brick or some other heavy object a short distance beyond the end of the incline. Place the doll on the car, truck, or roller skate and let the vehicle with its "passenger" roll down the incline and collide with the brick. What happens to the vehicle? What happens to the "passenger" when the vehicle crashes into the brick?

Repeat the experiment, but this time fasten the doll to the vehicle with strong, wide rubber bands, as shown in Figure 18. What happens to the passenger during the collision this time? Based on the results of this experiment, why do you think seat belts reduce deaths caused by traffic accidents?

Exploring on Your Own

How do Newton's first and second laws of motion apply to automobile accidents?

Design and carry out an experiment to show how the barrels of sand placed in front of concrete barriers at many exits from super-highways reduce the damage and loss of life that would occur if the cars collided with the concrete.

3

Balloons, Balls, Bounces, and Spins

You probably associate balloons with parties, and balls with such sports as basketball, tennis, softball, baseball, football, lacrosse, and golf. However, in this chapter you will see how balloons and balls can be used to investigate electricity, pressure, expansion and contraction of gases, elasticity, curveballs, and strange bounces that result from a combination of spin and friction.

3-1*
Electrical Balloons: Getting Charged Up

Electrical charges leak away quickly in warm, damp air; consequently, you should do this experiment on a winter day or a day when the humidity is low.

Long ago, scientists found that there are two kinds of charge, which they called positive and negative. It was Benjamin Franklin, one of the men who signed the Declaration of Independence, who established definitions of positive and negative charge. He defined glass that had been rubbed with silk, or anything repelled by the glass, to be positively charged. A rubber rod rubbed with wool, or anything repelled by the rubber rod, was said to have a negative charge. What kind of charge—positive or negative—do you think the silk had after it was used to rub the glass? What kind of charge do you think the wool had after it was used to rub the rubber?

You will find the answer to those questions and others in this experiment.

Blow up a balloon and hang it from a string. You can give the balloon a charge by rubbing it on your hair. After you have rubbed the balloon, what happens when you bring your hair near the balloon?

Now hang a second balloon from a string so that the two balloons hang side by side. Rub both balloons on your hair so that you give them both the same kind of charge. What do you notice about the balloons? Do they attract or repel each other? Do like charges attract or repel? Was the charge on your hair, which you used to charge the balloon, the same or opposite of the charge on the balloon? How do you know?

Things you will need:

- balloons
- string
- clear plastic tape
- ruler
- table
- puffed rice cereal
- bowl
- various other dry cereals
- Ping-Pong ball

You can charge two plastic strips of tape and determine the charge on each one. First, suspend a balloon from a string. Tape the end of the string to a door frame so the balloon hangs freely. Next, charge the balloon by rubbing it on your hair. Then tear off two 15-cm (6-in) strips of clear plastic tape. Fold one end of each strip so that you can grip the tape without having it adhere to your skin. Stick one strip of tape to the top of a clean table. Stick the second strip on top of the first one. Holding only the folded tape on the bottom strip, pull both pieces of tape off the table. Then use the folded ends to pull the two strips apart quickly.

Slowly bring first one strip and then the other close to the balloon. Do the strips carry the same or opposite charges? How do you know? How could you determine the sign (+ or −) of the charge on each strip?

Just for fun, pour a few pieces of puffed rice cereal into a bowl. Charge a balloon and hold it over the cereal. What happens? Since the puffed rice has not been charged, how can you explain what you observe?

Can you use a charged balloon to move other kinds of cereal? How can you use a charged balloon to make a Ping-Pong ball roll without touching it?

Exploring on Your Own

Investigate electrostatic induction. What is it? How is it related to what you observed with the puffed rice and the charged balloon? Design experiments to demonstrate electrostatic induction.

Investigate static charge as opposed to moving charge (current). How do they differ? How can each be obtained?

3-2*
Balloons, a Ping-Pong Ball, and Bernoulli

Eighteenth-century physicist and mathematician Daniel Bernoulli was able to show that as the velocity of a fluid (a liquid or a gas) increases, its pressure decreases. To see that this is true, use strings to hang two balloons side by side. The balloons should be several centimeters apart and motionless. What happens when you blow air between them? Can you explain why it happens?

Things you will need:

- 2 balloons
- string
- Ping-Pong ball
- hair dryer or a vacuum cleaner that will blow air
- flexible drinking straw
- tape
- thread
- kitchen faucet

Next, take a Ping-Pong ball and place it in a stream of air from a hair dryer or a vacuum cleaner that is connected so as to blow air out rather than suck it in. Can you explain why the ball stays in the airstream?

You can use your own lung power in place of the airstream from a vacuum cleaner or a hair dryer. Hold a Ping-Pong ball over the end of a flexible straw that points straight up, as shown in Figure 19. Blow air as hard as you can through the straw. At the moment you start blowing, release the ball. You will find that it will remain in the airstream for as long as you continue to blow high-speed air through the straw.

Will high-speed water produce the same low pressure as fast-moving air? To find out, use a small piece of tape to attach a piece of thread to a Ping-Pong ball. Bring the ball close to a stream of water flowing from a kitchen faucet. What happens? How can you tell there is a force pulling on the ball? Do you get a similar effect if you bring a balloon suspended from a string close to the fast-moving stream of water?

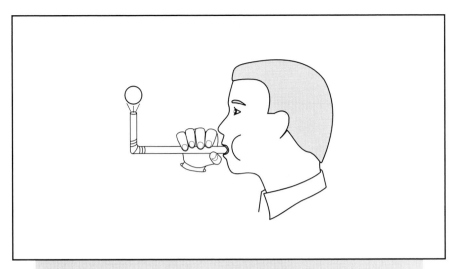

Figure 19. You can use your lung power to keep a Ping-Pong ball in a fast-moving airstream.

What is the source of the force that holds objects in a fast-flowing stream of fluid?

Exploring on Your Own

Write a short biography about Daniel Bernoulli, highlighting his contributions to science.

What is Bernoulli's principle and what is its significance?

3-3*
Balloons: Hot and Cold

Pull the neck of a balloon over the mouth of each of two empty 1- or 2-liter glass or rigid plastic bottles. Put one bottle in the refrigerator. Put the other bottle in a pan of hot water.

Watch what happens to the balloon on the bottle that was placed in hot water. What do your observations tell you? What effect does temperature have on the volume of a gas?

After a few minutes, predict what you think the balloon on the bottle you put in the refrigerator will look like. Then, open the refrigerator and look. What has happened to the balloon? Does what you observe agree with your prediction?

Put the bottle and balloon that was in the hot water in a freezer. What do you think will happen to the balloon? What do you think will happen to the balloon on the bottle that was in the refrigerator if you place the bottle in hot water?

Things you will need:

- 2 balloons
- two 1- or 2-liter glass or rigid plastic bottles
- refrigerator
- pan of hot water

Exploring on Your Own

Design and carry out an experiment to find out by what fraction of its original volume a gas expands or contracts with each degree Celsius change in temperature.

3-4
A Balloon in a Bottle

Place all but the mouth of a balloon inside a rigid plastic bottle. (The bottle must be hard plastic, not the soft plastic in ordinary soda bottles.) Pull the mouth of the balloon over the opening at the top of the bottle, as shown in Figure 20. Try to inflate the balloon by blowing into it. Why can't you fill the balloon with air?

Things you will need:
- balloon
- rigid plastic bottle (pint-size)
- an adult
- nail or drill to make a hole in the bottle
- unsharpened pencil

Ask an adult to punch or drill a hole in the side of the bottle near its bottom. Now you will find that you can inflate the balloon. Why can you inflate the balloon now that the bottle has a hole in it?

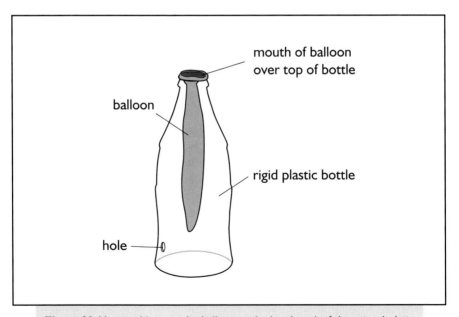

Figure 20. You can blow up the balloon in the bottle only if there is a hole in the bottle.

Inflate the balloon and then put your thumb over the hole near the bottom of the bottle. As you can see, the balloon remains inflated even when you remove your mouth from the balloon. How can the balloon remain inflated when its mouth is open to the air?

You can use the balloon as a "rocket launcher." Blow up the balloon, and then put your thumb firmly over the hole in the bottle. **Keeping your head away from the bottle,** put an unsharpened pencil into the balloon. **Continue to keep your head away from the bottle** as you remove your thumb. The balloon will contract and launch the pencil into the air.

3-5*
Superball and Other Bouncers

One of the features of a Superball is its "bounciness." But just how bouncy is it and how does its bounciness compare with the same property in other balls you use in games?

To find out, ask a friend to hold a meterstick or yardstick upright on a hard floor or sidewalk, as shown in Figure 21. Hold a Superball so that the bottom of the ball is level with the top of the measuring stick. Then drop the ball. Have your friend watch to see how high the Superball bounces after it hits the floor or sidewalk. Should your friend measure the height from the bottom or top of the ball? Why?

Things you will need:

- yardstick or meterstick
- hard floor or sidewalk
- Superball
- a friend
- rubber ball
- Styrofoam ball
- clay
- notebook
- pen or pencil
- balls used in a variety of sports, such as baseball, softball, Ping-Pong, basketball, golf, handball, lacrosse, soccer, squash, tennis, etc.

Repeat the experiment several times. Does the ball bounce to very nearly the same height each time? In your notebook, record the average height to which the Superball bounces. To what fraction of its original height does it bounce?

Repeat the experiment with a rubber ball, a Styrofoam ball, and a ball made from clay. To what fraction of the drop height does each ball rise after bouncing? How does the bounciness of these balls compare with that of a Superball?

Repeat the experiment with a number of balls used in different games, such as baseball, softball, tennis, basketball, lacrosse, soccer, golf, and so on. Which of the game balls you tested bounced the most? The least? Did any come close to the Superball in its bounce?

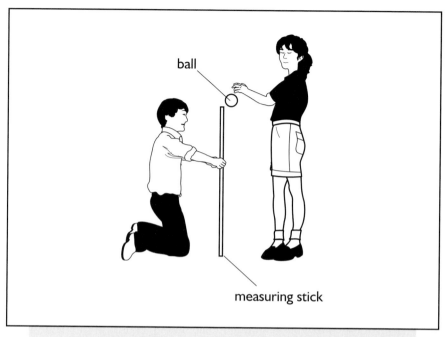

ball

measuring stick

Figure 21. How does the bounce of different balls compare?

Does the surface from which a ball bounces affect the height to which it rises after bouncing? To find out, drop a Superball and several other balls used in games onto different surfaces, such as wood, concrete, tile, macadam, carpet, grass, and soil. From your results, can you find any way to predict how the bounce of a ball will be affected by the surface onto which you drop it?

Exploring on Your Own

Design and carry out an experiment to see if there is a relationship between the height to which a ball bounces and the number of previous bounces it has made after being dropped.

Design and carry out another experiment to see if the temperature of different balls has any effect on their bounciness.

Investigate the meaning of elastic and inelastic collisions. How are they related to the bounciness of the different balls you tested?

72

3-6*
Throwing Curves with a Beach Ball

A beach ball is easily moved by the wind. If you do this experiment outside, it should be done on a very calm day. If you do it inside, it should be done in the basement, garage, or a room where there is plenty of open space.

Things you will need:
- beach ball
- calm day, or a basement, garage, or room where there is plenty of open space
- baseball or softball pitcher
- baseball or softball
- tennis ball and racquet
- basketball

Hold the beach ball in both hands and launch it forward without any spin. The ball will travel in a straight line, but will, of course, fall to the floor.

Next, launch the ball forward, but give it a clockwise spin as seen by you (Figure 22a). Repeat the experiment several times and watch the ball carefully. Does it curve to the right or to the left as it moves forward?

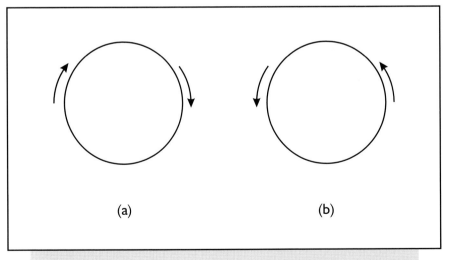

(a)   (b)

Figure 22. The arrows show the direction of rotation as seen by a person who launches a ball with: a) clockwise spin; b) counterclockwise spin.

Now launch the ball so that it has a counterclockwise spin (Figure 22b). Do this several times. Which way does the ball curve now?

If you hold the ball with the tips of your fingers, you can launch it with backspin, as shown in Figure 23a. This will affect the way it bounces. Can you give it enough backspin so that it will bounce back toward you after it hits the floor?

Can you predict what will happen if you launch the ball with topspin, as shown in Figure 23b? Try it! Were you right?

Ask a baseball or softball pitcher how he or she throws a curve-ball. Do they apply a spin to the ball? Does the ball they throw curve the way you would predict on the basis of the experiments you have done?

Can you make a tennis ball curve by hitting it with a racquet so that it spins clockwise or counterclockwise? Can you make a bas-ketball bounce differently by applying backspin or topspin?

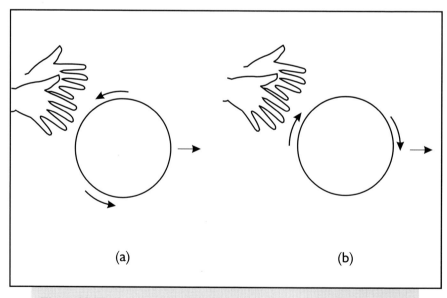

(a)   (b)

Figure 23. The balls being launched forward are shown from a side view. In (a) the ball is launched with backspin. In (b) the ball is being launched with topspin.

Exploring on Your Own

Some people claim the curveball baseball pitchers throw is really an optical illusion. Design an experiment to find out if a baseball really can be made to curve. Then, **under adult supervision**, and with the help of a curveball pitcher, carry out your experiment. What do you find?

When basketball players launch a jump shot, what kind of spin do they put on the ball? Is this spin useful in helping to make the ball go through the hoop?

4

Bring in the Artillery and Rockets

No, this chapter is not about war, guns, and missiles. But it does involve the use of toy water pistols and pressurized water guns as well as water "bombs," toy rockets, and orbiting marbles. You will find that these toys can serve as a basis for experiments that will help you to understand how and why things move, ascend, fall, or orbit the earth.

4-1*
The Speed and Range of Water Projectiles

Although real guns are deadly and very dangerous, you can learn a lot about science by shooting water guns and water pistols. One of your favorite toys on a warm summer day may be a water pistol or a water gun. The cool water is harmless and feels good when it hits your warm skin. In this experiment, you will find out how fast these water projectiles travel and how they can be "fired" to achieve maximum range.

How Fast Do Water Projectiles Travel?

Place a filled water pistol near the edge of a picnic table or some other elevated supporting surface. If possible, set the barrel of the water pistol at a height of approximately 1 meter or 1 yard above a long level surface such as a walk, driveway, or the floor of a garage, barn, basement, long hallway, or another place that has a surface that will not be damaged by water.

Things you will need:

- water
- water pistol
- picnic table or some other raised level support
- meterstick or yardstick
- long level surface, such as a walk, driveway, or the floor of a garage, barn, basement, or long hallway
- carpenter's level
- marking pen
- plumb bob
- measuring tape
- calculator
- 2 coins
- ruler
- table
- air gun that uses pressurized air to propel water
- suction-cup tipped darts and dart gun
- protractor
- sheet of cardboard
- a partner

Use a carpenter's level to be sure the gun barrel is level, then pull the trigger and mark the point where the most distant drop lands. Use a plumb bob, such as the one shown in Figure 24, to mark

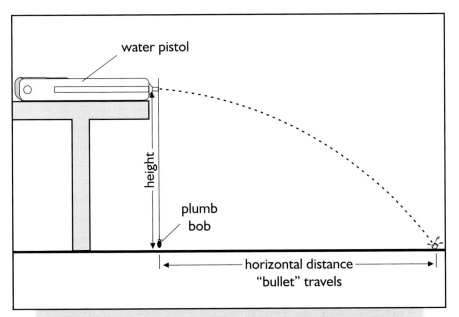

water pistol

height

plumb
bob

horizontal distance
"bullet" travels

Figure 24. A water projectile's horizontal speed can be determined experimentally. The horizontal distance from the bottom of the plumb bob to the projectile's landing point gives the distance the projectile traveled horizontally. The time to fall a known height can be calculated. Dividing the distance by the time will give the projectile's horizontal speed.

a point directly below the end of the gun barrel. Measure the distance between the point on the floor beneath the end of the barrel and the point where the most distant water drop landed. That measurement is the horizontal distance the projectile traveled after it left the gun barrel.

If you know the time for the projectile to travel from the barrel to the ground, you can calculate its horizontal speed. Speed is equal to distance divided by time. Because all objects (where air resistance is negligible) fall with the same acceleration, the time to fall 1 meter or 1 yard can be determined. It takes an object 0.45 second to fall 1 meter and 0.43 second to fall 3 feet or 1 yard. In that time, the water projectile traveled the horizontal distance you measured.

If you cannot place the water pistol at a height of very nearly 1 meter or 1 yard, you can calculate the time to reach the floor from any height. If the distance the water traveled is measured in meters, divide twice the height by 10 and find the square root of the quotient. If distance is measured in feet, divide twice the height by 32 and find the square root of the quotient.

Use the time and distance to calculate the horizontal speed of your water projectiles in meters per second (m/s) or feet per second (ft/s). How fast do they travel? What is their speed in kilometers per hour (kph) or miles per hour (mph)?

The information that you used to calculate the horizontal speed of a projectile is based on an assumption. The assumption is this: If one projectile is dropped from the same height and at the same time that a second projectile is fired horizontally from the barrel of a gun, both projectiles will reach the ground at the same time.

You can test this assumption quite easily. Place two coins and a ruler at the edge of a table, as shown in Figure 25. Strike the ruler sharply at the point indicated by the arrow. The inertia (resistance to motion) of the coin resting on the ruler will cause it to remain in place as the ruler moves out from under it, and it will fall straight down to the floor. At the same moment, the coin on the table will be projected horizontally when the other side of the ruler strikes it. Listen carefully. You will hear the two coins hit the floor at the same time.

With the more expensive water guns, air is pumped into the gun and the pressurized air is used to propel the water projectiles. What is the speed of the air-driven water that emerges from these water guns?

You can use the same kind of experiment to measure the horizontal speed of the rubber suction-cup tipped projectiles from a dart gun. How do the speeds of the dart gun and squirt gun projectiles compare?

What Is the Range of a Squirt Gun?

If a friend runs away from you to get beyond the range of your squirt gun's projectiles, what can you do to increase the range of your gun?

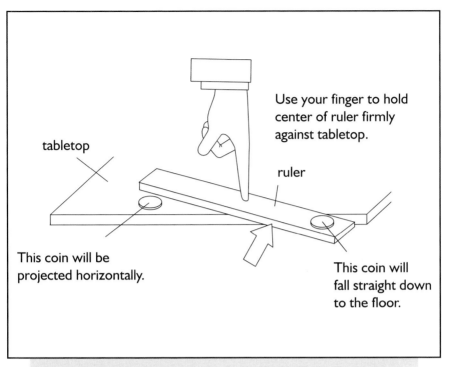

Use your finger to hold center of ruler firmly against tabletop.

tabletop

ruler

This coin will be projected horizontally.

This coin will fall straight down to the floor.

Figure 25. This experiment will show that a projectile fired horizontally and another dropped at the same time from the same height will reach the floor at the same time.

One approach might be to change the angle at which you shoot the water.

To see how firing angle affects the range of a squirt gun, you can shoot the projectiles at different angles and see where they land. The firing angle can be measured by using a large protractor.

Use a sheet of cardboard to build a large half-protractor, as shown in Figure 26. Place the giant protractor on a level surface, such as a floor, walk, or driveway. Have a friend mark the point where the farthest drop of water lands when the water pistol is fired horizontally from the top of the protractor.

After marking the range for 0 degrees, launch the water at an angle of 10 degrees. Be sure the end of the water gun's barrel is at

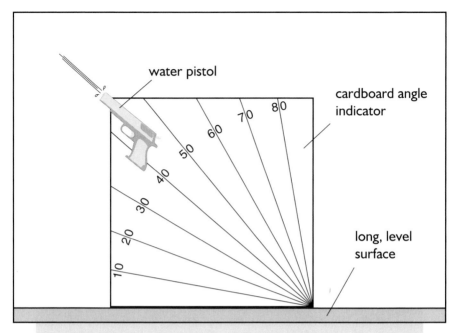

Figure 26. A water pistol is "fired" at various angles, using a cardboard half-protractor. At what angle does the gun have its maximum range?

the same height above the level surface as it was when you fired the water horizontally (at 0 degrees).

Again, have a partner mark the point where the farthest drop of water lands. The distance from the launch site to the point where the water lands is the range for that angle. Repeat the experiment at angles of 20, 25, 30, 35, 40, 45, 50, 55, 60, 65, 70, 75, and 80 degrees. Where will the drops land if you fire the gun at a 90-degree angle?

At what angle is the gun's range a maximum? Are there angles for which the range is very nearly or exactly the same? If there are, what are these angles?

Determine the maximum range for the more expensive water guns in which air is pumped into the gun and the pressurized air is used to propel the water projectiles. Does this kind of gun achieve its maximum range at the same angle as the water pistol?

Exploring on Your Own

Design and carry out an experiment to determine the acceleration at which all objects (where air resistance is negligible) fall when close to the earth's surface.

Using physics and mathematics, show that the theoretical maximum range of a projectile occurs when the projectile is fired at an angle of 45 degrees.

4-2*
Water "Bombs" Away!

Planes dropping food, water, and medical supplies to people stranded by floods, earthquakes, and other natural disasters must know when to release their cargo. When should it be dropped so that it will land where people can reach it?

Things you will need:
- bicycle
- level sidewalk, path, or driveway
- water
- balloons
- chalk
- tennis ball

The challenge of dropping objects onto a target from a moving plane is related to Newton's first law of motion, which states that a body in motion will maintain its motion unless acted upon by a force. It is also related to Newton's second law of motion: When a force acts on a body, the body accelerates in the direction of the force. The body's acceleration is proportional to the force; that is, doubling the force will double the acceleration. The acceleration is also inversely proportional to the mass of the body; doubling the mass will halve the acceleration. In the case of falling objects, the force is gravity and all objects fall with the same acceleration because the force of gravity is proportional to the mass of the falling object.

To investigate the problem of hitting a target from a moving object, you can use your bicycle, a level sidewalk, path, or drive-way, and some water cargo. You can make the water cargo by filling balloons with water and sealing them. Use some chalk to make a target on the sidewalk, path, or driveway.

Now hold the balloon against one handle of your bicycle (Figure 27) as you ride over the target. Try to aim your bike so that the cargo will pass directly over the target. At the moment the cargo is above the target release it. Does it hit the target, or does it land some other place? Where should you release the cargo so that it lands on the target?

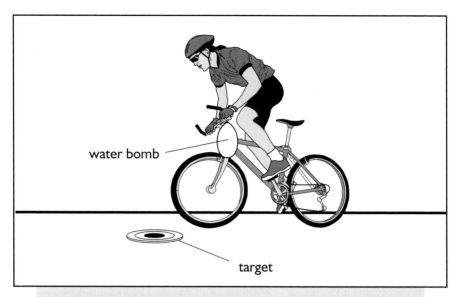

Figure 27. A water-bombing cyclist is shown taking aim at a target.

Does changing the speed of your bicycle change the point at which you must release the cargo to score a hit? If so, how does it change the release point?

What is involved in releasing cargo from a moving vehicle so that it will hit a target on the ground below?

A simple experiment related to hitting targets from a moving vehicle can be done by dropping a tennis ball as you walk along a floor. Drop the ball as you walk at a normal pace. Can you catch the ball as it rebounds while you are still walking? Does the ball continue to move forward after you drop it?

Next, drop the tennis ball and immediately stop walking at the moment you release it. Does the ball stop moving forward or does it continue to move on ahead of you?

Exploring on Your Own

Design and carry out an experiment to map the path of an object, such as a water balloon dropped from a bike, that is moving horizontally as it falls from a height. What is the shape of its path? How can its path be explained?

4-3*
Ascending Rockets: To What Height?

The motion of rockets, missiles, airplanes, boats, cars, even walkers and cyclists is related to Newton's third law of motion. The law states that for every force there is always an equal and opposite force. This might be called the "push, push back" law. If I push on you, you automatically push back on me with an equal force in the opposite direction.

To see how the push, push back law works, ask a friend to join you on ice skates, roller skates, or in-line skates. Both you and your friend should be at rest with you standing behind and close to your friend. Tell your friend that you are going to give him or her a push. Then do so. It probably comes as no surprise to see your friend move away from you. But notice that you are moving in the opposite direction. Your friend automatically pushed back on you when you pushed forward on him or her.

Things you will need:

- a friend
- ice skates, roller skates, or in-line skates
- medicine ball
- plastic drinking straw
- thread
- oblong balloon
- twist-tie
- tape
- lightweight plastic truck
- smooth, level surface
- toy rocket that uses air under pressure to force water out its nozzle
- cardboard
- pen
- protractor
- ruler
- string
- pin
- a weight, such as lead sinker, steel washer, or nut
- large open field
- measuring tape
- large sheet of paper

What happens if you repeat the experiment on someone who is much heavier than you? What happens if you repeat the experiment on someone who is much lighter than you? What happens if, while on skates, you push on something firmly fastened to the earth, such as a tree or the boards around a hockey or roller skating rink?

Rockets

Rockets are based on Newton's third law of motion. In order to move forward, something inside the rocket is pushed out the back. In the case of real rockets, such as those used to launch the space shuttle, hot fuel is ejected from a nozzle at the rear of the rocket. The fuel pushed out the back exerts an equal but opposite push on the rocket, causing it to move forward or up.

You can be a one-shot rocket. All you need is a heavy object such as a medicine ball and some ice skates, roller skates, or in-line skates. While standing on the skates, push the medicine ball away from you as hard as you can without falling. In which direction do you move?

You can make a balloon rocket by mounting a plastic drinking straw on a thread, as shown in Figure 28a. Tie one end of the thread to a heavy object near the floor. Tie the other end to a tall object on the opposite side of the room.

Blow up an oblong balloon, seal its neck with a twist-tie, and tape it to the straw, as shown in Figure 28b. Move the balloon to a point near the lower end of the long string. Then carefully remove the twist-tie with one hand while keeping the neck of the balloon closed with the other. What happens when you release the balloon? Which way is air pushed out the neck of the balloon? Which way is the balloon pushed? What is the balloon rocket's fuel? What happens when the balloon rocket runs out of fuel?

Rockets are used to lift the space shuttle into orbit. In a similar way, a balloon rocket can be used to put other vehicles into motion. Use tape to attach a large balloon to a lightweight plastic truck, as shown in Figure 29. You will find that air ejected backward from

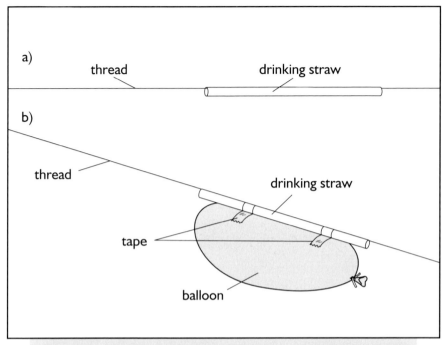

Figure 28. a) To make a balloon rocket: (a) mount a drinking straw on a long thread. b) Use tape to attach a balloon to the straw. What happens when the balloon is released?

the balloon will cause the truck to move forward along a smooth, level surface.

At a toy or novelty store, you can buy a rocket that is launched by using air under pressure to force water out the rocket's nozzle. If you follow the directions provided with the rocket, you will find that it will ascend high into the air.

How High Will the Rocket Ascend?

You have seen that the toy rocket powered by pressurized air and water will ascend quite high into the air. But how high does it rise?

To find out, you can build an astrolabe that will allow you to measure the angle between the rocket and the ground when the rocket reaches its maximum altitude.

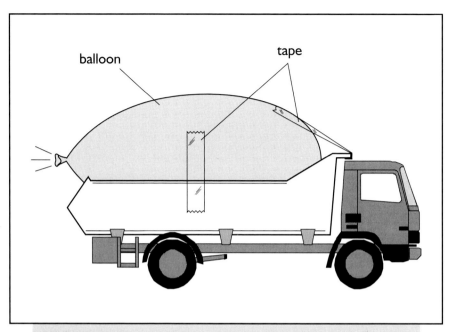

Figure 29. A balloon rocket can be used to put a lightweight toy truck into motion.

Figure 30 shows you how to build the astrolabe from a square sheet of cardboard. Degree lines can be marked using a pen, protractor, and ruler. One end of a string is tied to a pin that is stuck through the point where all the degree lines meet. The other end is tied to a weight.

In an open field, stand a known distance from the launch site where a friend will launch the rocket straight up into the air. A distance of about 50 meters or 50 yards is probably good, but you may have to adjust the distance. Try to find a distance that does not produce very large (70–90°) or very small (0–20°) angles.

You can follow the upward path of the rocket by sighting along the upper edge of the astrolabe as the rocket ascends to its maximum height. The weighted string will mark the angle between the rocket and an imaginary horizontal line at the height of your eyes. When the rocket reaches its peak height, press the string against

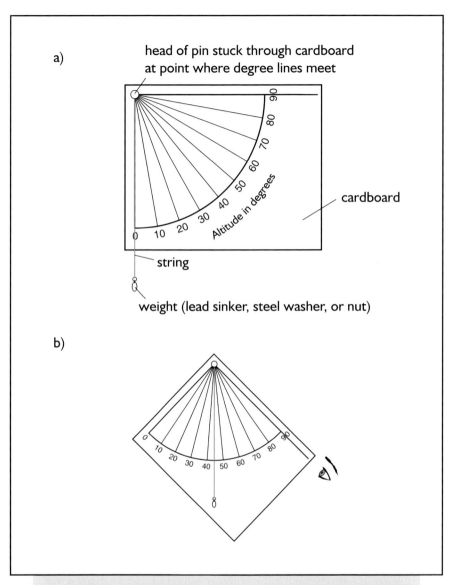

Figure 30. a) An astrolabe, which is used to measure angles, can be made from a square sheet of cardboard, a pin, string, and a weight. A protractor can be used to mark the degree lines. The 90°-line should be parallel to the top edge of the cardboard. The 0°-line should be parallel to the front edge of the astrolabe. b) When used to track the rocket, the string will indicate the rocket's angular altitude.

the dial on the cardboard. You can determine the rocket's angular altitude by the string, which will indicate the angle.

Knowing the angle and your distance from the launch site, you can draw a triangle, like the one shown in Figure 31, on a large sheet of paper. The base of the triangle is the known distance from the launch site to the point where you stood to measure the angle to the rocket at its maximum height. If you were 50 meters from the launch, you might let 1.0 cm on your scaled drawing represent 5.0 m of distance. In that case, the base of the triangle you draw would be 10 cm long because

$$50 \text{ m} \times 1.0 \text{ cm}/5.0 \text{ m} = 10 \text{ cm}.$$

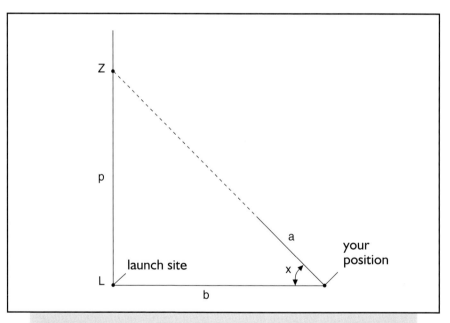

Figure 31. The base of the triangle, *b*, represents the distance between the launch site, *L*, and the point where you measured the angular altitude of the rocket. The line *p*, which is perpendicular to *b* at point *L*, represents the path of the rocket's upward flight. A short line, *a*, is drawn to show the angle, *x*, that you measured at the end of the base line, *b*. Line *a* is then extended until it meets line *p* at point *Z*. The scaled distance from *L* to *Z* represents the rocket's maximum height.

With a protractor you can draw the angle you measured at one end of the base line. At the other end of the base line, use a ruler and protractor to draw a line of indefinite length that is perpendicular (90°) to the base line. The perpendicular line represents the upward flight of the rocket.

Extend the angle line until it meets the line representing the rocket's upward path. How can you use the triangle you have drawn and the distance of your eye from the ground to determine the rocket's maximum height? What was the rocket's maximum height? What assumptions have you made?

What can you do to reduce or increase the rocket's maximum height?

Exploring on Your Own

Under adult supervision, build a rocket that uses a chemical fuel. To what height does it ascend?

Investigate the various rockets used to carry payloads into space.

Learn the history of the NASA space shuttle.

Research NASA's plans for a space station and additional space explorations.

4-4*
A Marble in Orbit

Once rockets have lifted the space shuttle into orbit, it goes around the earth as much as any near-earth satellite. Gravity provides the inward (centripetal) force that keeps pulling the ship inward. As a result, the space shuttle moves along a path that carries it around the earth about once every 90 minutes. The moon, which is much farther away than the space shuttle and other man-made satellites, also orbits the earth. Because it is so much farther away, it takes the moon nearly a month to orbit the earth. On an even larger scale, the earth and the other eight planets are satellites that orbit the sun. In all these cases, it is gravity that provides the centripetal force needed to keep the satellites in orbit.

Things you will need:

- glass marble
- clear, round, plastic cake-dish cover
- large plastic snap-on cover (one used on 39-oz coffee can is good)
- scissors

What would happen if gravity could be turned off? Newton had an answer to that question. Do you?

One way to find out is to place a large marble inside a clear, round, plastic cake-dish cover, like the one shown in Figure 32a. If you gently swirl the clear plastic cover in small circles on a floor or table, a glass marble inside the dish will go into "orbit." In this case, the side of the cover provides the centripetal force needed to keep the marble moving along its orbit. If you stop moving the cake cover, the marble will continue to move in a circle for a while. Can you explain why?

Put the marble back into orbit. Once it is moving smoothly in a circle, lift one side of the cake cover. Which of the paths shown in Figure 32b does the marble follow when "gravity" is turned off?

Here is another way to observe the path a satellite would follow if gravity could be turned off. Place the marble inside the lip of

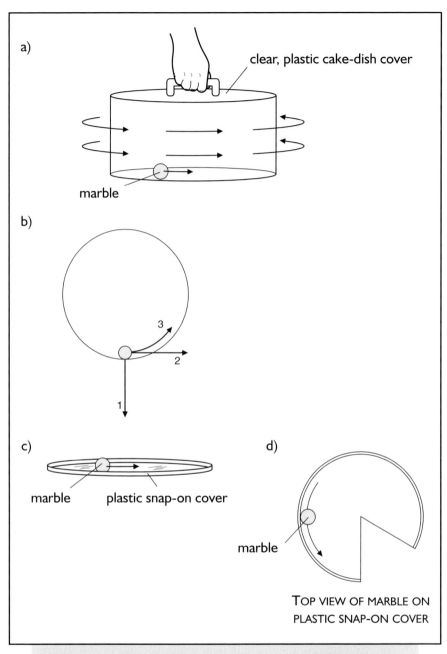

Figure 32. a) Using a clear, plastic cake-dish cover, put a marble into "orbit." b) If the inward force keeping the marble in orbit is removed, along which path (1,2, or 3) will the marble travel? c) This marble is orbiting a large plastic snap-on cover. d) When the marble reaches the cutaway section, which of the paths shown in (b) will it follow?

a large plastic snap-on cover. Give the marble a push so that it moves in a circular fashion about the inside circumference of the lid, as shown in Figure 32c. What provides the centripetal force that keeps the marble in orbit?

To see what happens when the centripetal force is removed, cut away a section of the cover, as shown in Figure 32d. Start the marble in motion along the rim of the lid. What happens when the centripetal force holding it in orbit is removed? Which of the paths shown in Figure 32b does it follow? Can you explain why?

Exploring on Your Own

Investigate what are called geostationary orbits. Why are some satellites placed in geostationary orbits?

Apollo spacecraft were used by NASA to send astronauts to the moon. How were they able to reach the moon? Why didn't they, like the space shuttle, stay in orbit around the earth?

Investigate ways being planned to send manned spaceships to Mars.

Explain how Newton's first law of motion is related to Experiment 4-4.

Science with a Variety of Toys

In this final chapter you will have an opportunity to use a variety of toys to do more experiments. Experimentation is the backbone of science. You will use wagons to investigate wheels, circles, and how wheels can be used to measure distance. You will see how forces affect the speed of wagons and how weight, force, and acceleration are related. You can investigate the variables that affect the drinking rate of a toy dipping bird, try to determine what makes objects sink or float, figure out a way to estimate the thickness of something as thin as a soap bubble, find out how a Push-N-Go® toy works, and compare the walking speed of a wind-up toy with your own walking speed.

5-1*
Circling Wagons on the Move

Can you think of some wheels that turn around but do not go anywhere? You can probably name some of them. Did you think of the giant Ferris wheels you find in amusement parks? How about the steering wheels on cars, the gears in a watch, clock, or automobile transmission, or the pulley wheels on electric motors or gasoline engines?

In this investigation you will focus on wheels that roll along the ground as they turn. These are the wheels you find on bicycles, cars, trains, roller skates, and wagons. Such wheels are usually attached to a rod called an axle.

Look at the wheels on a child's wagon. Are they firmly fixed to the axle so that both wheels turn together? Or can one wheel turn without turning the axle and the other wheel?

Pull a wagon around a circular path. Does the outside wheel go around the same number of times as the inside wheel attached to the same axle? To find out, put a piece of tape on each wheel. This will help you to count the number of times each wheel goes around. You may find it useful to have a friend count the rotations of the outside wheel while you count those of the inside wheel. Does the inside wheel rotate more, fewer, or the same number of times as the outside wheel? Which wheel travels farther?

Things you will need:
- child's wagon
- tape
- a friend
- marking pen, chalk, or other means of marking one of the wagon's tires and sidewalk or path
- cloth tape measure
- parent
- pen or pencil
- notebook
- cardboard
- scissors or shears
- long sheet of wrapping paper
- wall
- various wheels and other circular objects, such as tin cans, oatmeal boxes, large coins or washers, etc.
- basketball

Can you pull the wagon in a circle so that the inside wheel does not turn at all? If the wheels were fixed to the axle so that both axle and wheels turned together, what would happen when you pulled the wagon in a circle with a small diameter?

When the wheels on your wagon go around once, how far does the wagon move forward? To find out, make a mark on one of the wagon's tires at the point where the tire touches the ground. Make a second mark on the sidewalk or path where the tire is touching, as shown in Figure 33a. Pull the wagon straight ahead until the tire has gone around once. Make a second mark on the ground where the tire touches the ground (see Figure 33b).

How can you find the distance the wheel moved along the ground? Is it the same distance the whole wagon moved?

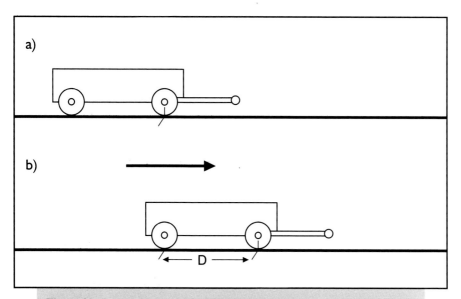

Figure 33. a) A mark is made or placed on the wagon's tire at the point where the tire touches the ground. A second mark is made on the ground directly beneath the mark on the tire. b) The wagon is pulled forward until the wheel has made one complete rotation. A new mark is made on the ground at the point directly beneath the mark on the tire. What does the distance D between the two marks on the ground represent?

Use a tape measure to determine the wheel's circumference (the distance around it). How does the wheel's circumference compare with the distance the wheel rolled forward? How can you use your wagon to measure distances?

With your parent's permission, use your wagon and the information you have collected to measure the distance between your home and the home of a friend. If you can walk to your school, use your wagon to find the distance between your home and your school.

A Bug on a Wheel

If you were a tiny bug riding on the outside rim of a rolling wheel, what kind of a path would you follow? Do you think it would be a circle? If you do, think again!

To find the actual path in which the bug would travel, make a mark on the outside rim of a wagon wheel. Then watch the mark as someone else pulls the wagon slowly forward. Can you see what kind of a path the mark follows?

A better way is to map the path of a point on a rolling wheel. You can do this quite easily by making a large cardboard circle to represent a wheel. Use a pencil to punch a hole through the cardboard near the outer edge of the "wheel." Put a pencil point through the hole. Then roll the wheel slowly along the floor next to a long sheet of wrapping paper taped to a wall (see Figure 34). The pencil point will map the path the bug on the rim would follow. How would you describe the path?

What path would the bug follow if it were at the center of the wheel? If it were halfway between the center and the rim of the wheel?

Circumference to Diameter: An Interesting Ratio

Use a cloth tape measure to find the diameter of a wheel—the distance from one edge of the wheel across its center to the opposite edge. Then measure the circumference of the wheel—the distance

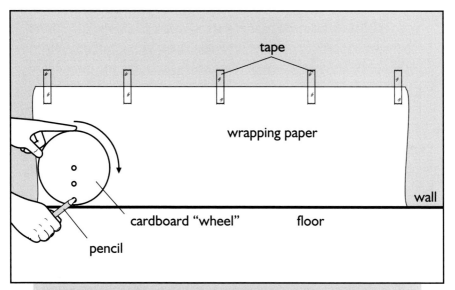

Figure 34. A cardboard wheel is rolled along a floor. The path a bug on the wheel would follow is marked on wrapping paper taped to a wall.

around its outside edge. Do the same thing with a number of other circular objects with different diameters, such as other wheels, tin cans, oatmeal boxes, large coins or washers, and so on. Record the circumference and diameter of each circular object you measure. Then divide the circumference of each one by its diameter. How do these ratios compare with one another?

Now measure the diameter of a wheel you have not measured before. Predict the distance the wheel will travel forward in one rotation. Try it! Were you right?

Predict the diameter of a basketball by measuring its largest circumference. How can you measure the diameter of the basketball to see if your prediction was right?

Exploring on Your Own

How can you make a set of wheels attached to an axle that will always roll in a circle? How can you control the radius of the circular path made by the wheels?

With a mechanic's permission, look at the wheels on a car that has been raised on a lift at a gas station or garage where cars are repaired or serviced. **Be sure an adult is standing by.** In cars with front-wheel drive, the front wheels seem to be attached to the same axle, while the rear wheels rotate on separate axles. The reverse is true of cars with rear-wheel drive. The bump on the axle between the two wheels that seem to be attached to the same axle houses the car's differential. Investigate how the differential works. What purpose does it serve? What would happen to a car if the wheels were fixed to the same axle and there were no differential?

5-2*
Pulling Wagons

Normally, you pull a child's wagon along at a constant speed and pay little attention to the force with which you pull it. But in this experiment, you will measure the force and see what effect different forces have on the wagon when it is loaded in different ways.

To begin, place a weight in the wagon. You might use a concrete block, a pail of sand, or some other heavy object that can be easily duplicated. Use a 0–2,000 g (0–20 newton) spring scale to move the wagon along a smooth, level surface at a slow, constant speed.

Things you will need:
- child's wagon
- concrete block, a pail of sand, or some other heavy object that can be easily duplicated
- 0–2,000 g (0–20 newton) spring scale
- smooth, level surface
- measuring tape
- stopwatch or watch with a second hand

What is the reading on the spring scale when the wagon moves at a steady speed? This reading is a measure of the frictional force between the wheels and the surface. A frictional force is a force that acts against the motion of an object as it rolls or slides over a surface.

What happens when the force you apply to the wagon is less than the frictional force?

What happens when the force you use to pull the wagon is greater than the frictional force? To find out, use the spring scale to pull the wagon with a force twice as large as the frictional force. Keep the spring stretched to that force as you pull the wagon along the smooth, level surface. What happens to the wagon's speed as you continue to pull it with this constant force?

What do you think will happen if you use the spring scale to apply a force four times as large as the frictional force acting against the wagon's motion? Try it! Were you right?

Now double the weight in the wagon by adding a second concrete block, pail of sand, or whatever you are using as weights. Does the weight affect the friction between the wagon's wheels and the surface over which it moves? How can you find out?

Now pull on this heavier wagon with the same *net* force you applied to the lighter wagon. For example, if you pulled on the wagon with a force 2.0 newtons (200 g) greater than the force of friction when you had one unit of weight in the wagon, do the same now that there are two units of weight in the wagon. That is, pull with a force 2.0 newtons greater than the frictional force on the wagon or with whatever force greater than friction you used when the wagon had one unit of weight in it. You want the net force—the total force applied less the frictional force—to be the same as it was for one unit of weight in the wagon.

Does the added weight of the wagon affect the rate at which the wagon's speed increases under the same force? If so, how does it affect it?

You have seen that the wagon accelerates (continuously increases its speed) when you apply a force greater than the force of friction that opposes its motion. You have seen, too, that the acceleration is greater when the force is greater and smaller when the mass is increased. It is difficult to tell by simply observing whether or not an acceleration is constant—that is, whether or not the speed increases by the same amount during each succeeding second. However, it can be shown that if acceleration is constant, the distance traveled while accelerating will be proportional to the square of the time traveled. In other words, a wagon moving with constant acceleration will move four times as far in two units of time as it does in one unit of time. If it goes 2 meters in 2 seconds, it will go 8 meters in 4 seconds.

Design an experiment to find out if the wagon moves at constant acceleration when you apply a constant force. What do you find?

Exploring on Your Own

Using mathematics, show that if a body accelerates at a constant rate, its acceleration is proportional to the distance it travels and inversely proportional to the square of the time it takes to travel that distance. Then show that the acceleration is actually equal to twice the distance traveled divided by the square of the time to go that distance.

5-3

How Fast Does a Wind-Up Walking Toy Walk?

To find out how fast a wind-up walking toy walks, place a toy, such as the one shown in Figure 35, on a long, level floor. Be sure the toy will walk in a reasonably straight line. Then choose a starting point and place the toy there. Use a stick or something similar to mark the starting point. Place another marker several meters or yards away. It will serve as the finish line.

Have a friend with a stopwatch or a watch with a second hand or mode stand at the finish line. At the moment your friend says, "Go," release your walking

Things you will need:

- wind-up walking toys
- long, level floor
- sticks or similar markers
- meterstick or yardstick
- a friend
- stopwatch or a watch with a second hand or mode
- pen or pencil
- notebook
- wood, tile, linoleum, carpet, and other surfaces
- toy wind-up or pull-back cars
- open area where your walking and running speeds can be measured

toy at the starting point. Your friend will measure the time it takes the toy to walk the distance between the start and finish points.

Repeat the experiment several times to be sure the results are consistent. From the average time and the distance the toy traveled, determine the walking toy's average speed in centimeters per second (cm/s) or inches per second (in/s). At what speed does your walking toy move? Does the toy's speed decrease as it walks?

Does the surface on which your toy walks affect its speed? To find out, measure the toy's speed on wood, tile, linoleum, carpet, and other surfaces. What do you find?

Figure 35. How fast does a wind-up walking toy walk?

If possible, compare the speed of your walking toy with other walking toys. Compare your walking toy's speed with the speed of toy wind-up or pull-back cars.

How does the speed of these toys compare with the speed at which you normally walk? With the speed at which you normally run?

If you are willing to sacrifice one walking toy that belongs to you, see if you can figure out how it works.

5-4*
How Does a Push-N-Go® Toy Work?

Push-N-Go® is a Tomy toy that stores energy. You will need one for this experiment. The toy comes in several different forms. There is a fire engine, dump truck, and airplane. When you push down on the driver or pilot, you feel a force resisting your push. When you release your hand, the toy moves forward.

Things you will need:

- A Push-N-Go® toy
- screwdriver
- gears

How far will the toy go after you release it? Does the distance it travels depend on the surface over which it travels? Does it, for example, travel as far on a carpet as it does on a tile floor? If there are differences in the distance it travels on different surfaces, can you explain why?

What do you think makes the toy move after you release your hand? Develop a hypothesis (your own explanation) for how you think the toy works. Then, if the toy belongs to you, test your hypothesis by carefully taking the toy apart. All you need is a screwdriver to remove some screws. What do you find inside the toy? Can you explain how it works now?

If you have difficulty understanding how the gears inside the toy work, use some gears from a Lego® Technic set, or other gears you can find, to build a pair of gears such as the two shown in Figure 36a. When you turn gear A in a clockwise direction, which way does gear B turn? Suppose you have three gears, as shown in Figure 36b. Which way does gear C turn when gear A turns clockwise? When gear A turns counterclockwise, which way will gear C turn?

With the Push-N-Go® toy, notice what happens to the gears when you push down as opposed to what happens when you slowly release the spring.

How closely did your hypothesis of how the toy works compare with its actual working mechanism?

108

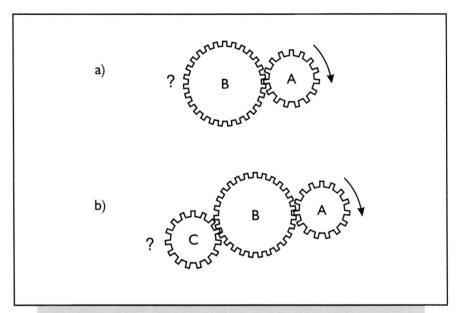

Figure 36. a) When gear A turns clockwise, which way does gear B turn? b) When gear A turns clockwise, which way does gear C turn?

When you push down on the Push-N-Go® toy, energy is stored in the toy. We say the toy has potential energy. In what form is the energy stored? To what form of energy is the stored energy converted?

Exploring on Your Own

Investigate some of the ways energy is converted from one form to another during your daily life. For example, what energy conversions take place when you ride your bike, throw a ball, or heat some water? On a larger scale, consider the energy conversions that take place, and where they take place, when you turn on a lightbulb.

5-5*
Why Does a Dipping Bird "Drink"?

You can buy a dipping or drinking bird like the one shown in Figure 37 in a toy or novelty store. If you put a container of water in front of the bird, will it start dipping its head and "drinking" the water? If not, what do you have to do to make the bird start dipping? Be sure the bird's beak can reach the water when it tips forward.

Things you will need:
- dipping bird (from a toy or novelty store)
- low plastic container
- clock or watch with a second hand
- small fan or open window
- small lightbulb and lamp
- hot tap water
- ice water
- rubbing alcohol

At what rate, in dips per minute, does your dipping bird "drink"? Can the bird's dipping rate be changed? Does it depend on the weather? For example, does the bird's dipping rate on a humid day differ from its dipping rate on a dry day if the temperature is the same?

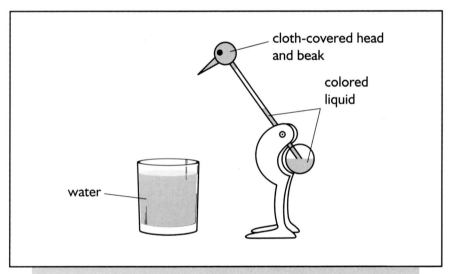

Figure 37. What makes a dipping bird "drink"?

What happens if you use a small fan or open window to provide the bird with a gentle breeze? Does the breeze affect the bird's dipping rate?

What happens if you place a small lightbulb near the bird in order to keep its head warm (**not hot**)? Does temperature affect the bird's dipping rate?

What happens if you give the bird hot tap water to "drink"? What happens if you give the bird ice water? Does the temperature of the water affect the bird's dipping rate?

Will its dipping rate be affected if you replace the water with rubbing alcohol?

Exploring on Your Own

Is the dipping bird a perpetual motion machine (one that goes forever)? Offer an experiment to support your answer.

Explain why the dipping bird "drinks." Then design and carry out experiments to test your explanation.

5-6*
Walking on Snow

If you live where winter brings ice and snow, you can use your sled, skis, toboggan, and snow-shoes to see how walking on snow is related to pressure.

Pressure is force per area. If a force of 500 newtons (N) pushes on an area of 100 square centimeters (cm^2), the pressure on that area is

Things you will need:

• deep snow

• sled, skis, toboggan, and snowshoes

• your shoes

• graph paper, with 1-cm squares

• pencil

• ruler

$$500 \text{ N} \div 100 \text{ cm}^2 = 5.0 \text{ N/cm}^2.$$

This means the force on each square centimeter is 5.0 newtons.

The same pressure can be expressed in pounds (lb) per square inch (in^2). Since 1.0 in^2 equals 6.45 cm^2 and 1.0 lb equals 4.54 N, that pressure would be

$$110 \text{ lb} \div 15.5 \text{ in}^2 = 7.1 \text{ lb/in}^2.$$

What pressure do you exert on the floor? To find out, place one of your shoes on a piece of graph paper that has 1-cm squares. Use a pencil to outline the shoe. If part of the shoe does not touch the paper, estimate that region of your shoe print and do not include it in your measurement of the area. The outline of your shoe on the graph paper will look like that in Figure 38a.

Add up the number of square centimeters within the outline of your shoe that touch the floor. Where the outline includes only portions of a square, add them together, as shown in Figure 38b.

What is the area of one of your shoes? On what total area does your weight rest? (Remember, you stand on two feet.) What pressure do you exert on the floor in newtons per square centimeter? In pounds per square inch?

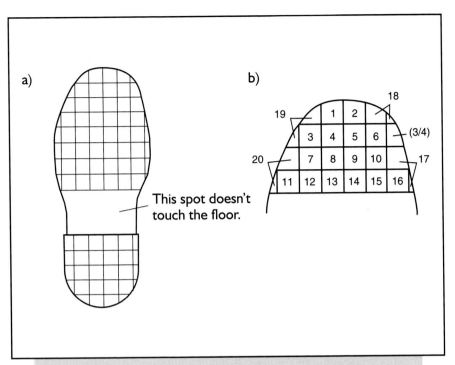

Figure 38. a) The outlined area of your shoe will be divided into square centimeters. b) Where only portions of squares lie within the outline, add them together as shown to obtain the best estimate of the area.

The pressure of the air is about 10 N/cm². Do you push on each square centimeter of floor with more or less pressure than the air?

Place your sled, skis, toboggan, and snowshoes on the snow. What area of each one is in contact with the snow? When you stand on the skis or snowshoes or sit on the sled or toboggan, what pressure do you exert on the snow?

Using the pressures you have calculated, which will sink farthest into the snow when you sit or stand on them: the sled, skis, toboggan, or snowshoes? Which will sink least into the snow? Is the depth to which the sled, skis, toboggan, or snowshoes sink into the snow proportional to the pressure they exert on the snow—that is, will the depth to which they sink double if the pressure doubles?

Exploring on Your Own

Why can someone wearing high-heel shoes make dents in a floor?

Why are smooth-soled sneakers often required wear for people playing on a tennis court?

A cubic meter of water weighs nearly 10,000 newtons. How deep does water have to be to exert a pressure equal to that of the air (10 N/cm^2)?

Investigate the ways in which air pressure can be measured.

5-7*
Clay, Boats, and Aluminum Beverage Cans

You have probably used clay to prepare sculpted models of animals and other things, but have you ever dropped a lump of clay into a container of water? If not, fill a plastic container with water. You can use a container like one that frozen whipped topping comes in. Then add the clay. As you can see, it sinks.

Now remove the clay and mold it into a boat. Can you make a boat that will float on the water? How much "cargo" will it carry? You can use coins as cargo.

Can you redesign the boat so that it will hold more cargo? If so, how did you change the boat?

Things you will need:
- clay
- plastic container (one that frozen whipped topping comes in works well)
- water
- coins
- toy wooden block
- empty aluminum soda can
- soda-filled aluminum can
- pail of water
- variety of beverage-filled aluminum cans
- small rubberized or ceramic magnet
- steel object such as a steel bolt
- aluminum foil or other aluminum object

Sink or Float

You found that clay sinks unless you sculpt it into a boat. Place a toy wooden block in water. Does it sink or float? Place some metal coins in water. Do they sink or float?

Place a variety of items on the surface of water. Which ones sink? Which ones float? Do you find a pattern that will allow you to predict which items will sink and which will float?

Find an empty aluminum soda can and one that is filled with soda. Open the full can and place the empty can beside it. Then fill the empty can with water until the level in the can is the same as the level in the full can you just opened.

Carefully place the can with water into a pail of water. Does it sink or float?

Obtain a variety of drinks in unopened 12-ounce aluminum cans. Try to include drinks that are carbonated and noncarbonated and drinks that are sugar-sweetened and artificially sweetened. If you have difficulty distinguishing aluminum cans from steel ones, use a small rubberized or ceramic magnet. Place the magnet near a steel object such as a steel bolt. Is a magnet attracted by steel? Now hold the magnet near a piece of aluminum foil or another aluminum object. Is a magnet attracted by aluminum? How can you use a magnet to distinguish aluminum cans from steel cans?

Place all the unopened cans containing drinks in a pail of water. To avoid trapping an air bubble in the can's concave bottom, put the cans in sideways and then turn them upright.

Which cans sink? Which cans float? Do you see any pattern that would enable you to predict which beverage can will sink and which will float?

Exploring on Your Own

Try to explain why some cans in the last experiment sink and others float. Then design and carry out an experiment to test your explanation.

During World War II, when there was a shortage of metals, some boats were built from concrete. Can you build a concrete boat that floats in water? You may need the help of an adult.

5-8*
How Thick Is a Soap Bubble?

Things you will need:
- tablespoon
- dishwashing liquid
- measuring cup
- soft water
- small plastic container with lid
- drinking straw
- bubble wand
- wire (optional)
- smooth counter
- meterstick or metric ruler
- pen or pencil
- notebook

Prepare a bubble solution by adding 1 tablespoon of dishwashing liquid to 1 cup of soft water. Pour the mixture into a container and stir it gently with a drinking straw to avoid making suds. Cover the solution and let it stand overnight.

Before you carry out an experiment to measure the thickness of a soap bubble, use the solution and a bubble wand to blow some bubbles. Most commercial bubble solutions come with a plastic wand. If you do not have such a wand, you can make one of your own by bending a wire into a circle. Leave some of the wire to serve as a handle.

Blow some bubbles and watch them as they sink slowly in the air. Notice the colors that appear on the soap film.

How can you prepare a wand that will allow you to make giant soap bubbles?

Pour some of the bubble solution you made onto a smooth counter. Using your hand, spread the solution over an area about 50 cm (20 in) across.

Dip a drinking straw into the solution that remains in the container. Lift the straw straight up from the solution and let any excess drain from the straw. Some liquid will remain in the end of the straw. Place the end of the straw and the solution that remains in it at the center of the wet area on the counter. Blow gently into the straw; the liquid that remains in the straw will form a bubble. Continue to blow until the bubble breaks. You will be amazed at the size of the hemispheric bubble you can make.

When the bubble breaks, it will leave a circle of droplets on the counter along its outside edge, or circumference. Use a meterstick or metric ruler to measure the diameter of the circle. What was the diameter of the bubble you blew with this solution?

Record this number in your notebook. Repeat the experiment several times to be sure the results are always about the same. What is the average diameter of the bubbles you blew?

Now you know the average diameter of the hemispherical bubbles. To find the thickness of the bubble, you need to know the volume of the solution you used to make the bubble. You can make a good estimate of the volume by using a ruler to measure the length (in millimeters) of the solution that remains in the straw after you let any excess solution drain from the straw (see Figure 39). You can also use the ruler to measure the diameter of the straw.

As you have seen, the bubble solution in the straw that you used to blow a bubble has a cylindrical shape. The volume of the liquid cylinder is equal to the area of its base times its height, or

$$\frac{1}{4}\pi d^2 h.$$

For example, suppose the length of the liquid in the straw was 1.0 mm and the diameter of the straw was 5.0 mm. The volume of the liquid would be

$$\frac{1}{4}\pi d^2 h = 0.25 \times 3.14 \times 25 \text{ mm}^2 \times 1.0 \text{ mm} = 20 \text{ mm}^3.$$

Suppose the bubble you blew had a diameter of 30 cm or 300 mm. All the bubble's volume would be contained in that bubble's surface area. Consequently, the surface area of the bubble times its average thickness, t, must equal the volume of the solution used to make the bubble. Since the surface area of a hemisphere is equal to $\frac{1}{2}d^2$, we can write

$$\frac{1}{2}\pi d^2 \times t = 20 \text{ mm}^3 \quad \text{or}$$

$$0.5 \times 3.14 \times 300 \text{ mm}^2 \times t = 20 \text{ mm}^3.$$

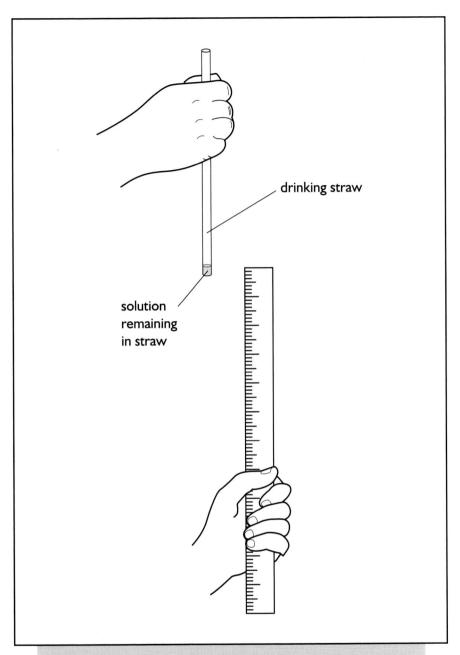

drinking straw

solution
remaining
in straw

Figure 39. Use a ruler to measure the height of the soap solution remaining in the straw. The same ruler can be used to measure the straw's diameter. From those two measurements, you can calculate the volume of the soap you will blow into a big bubble.

Since 0.5 x 3.14 x 300 mm^2 = 471 mm^2:

$$471 \text{ mm}^2 \times t = 20 \text{ mm}^3.$$

Divide both sides of the equation by 471 mm^2 to find the thickness:

$$t = 20 \text{ mm}^3 \div 471 \text{ mm}^2 = 0.042 \text{ mm}.$$

What is the average thickness of the bubbles you made?

Exploring on Your Own

Investigate why colors appear in soap bubbles when light shines on them.

In the experiment above, you measured the average thickness of a hemispheric soap bubble. Where is the bubble thickest? Where is it thinnest?

5-9*
Bubbles that Float

Prepare some bubble-making liquid and a bubble-making wand, as described in the previous experiment. Then pour about 2 cm (1 in) of water into a 4-liter (1-gal) plastic pail. Add about a dozen seltzer tablets to the water. The fizzing reaction

Things you will need:

• 4-liter (1-gal) plastic pail
• water
• seltzer tablets
• bubble wand
• bubble-making liquid

that you observe between the seltzer and the water is generating carbon dioxide gas.

Blow some bubbles with a wand. Let the bubbles fall into the pail. You may have to move the pail so it lies beneath a falling bubble. Will an air-filled bubble float on the carbon dioxide gas in the pail? What do your results tell you about the density of carbon dioxide as compared to the density of air?

Exploring on Your Own

Under adult supervision, design and carry out experiments to determine the density of air and carbon dioxide.

List of Suppliers

Carolina Biological Supply Co.
2700 York Road
Burlington, NC 27215
(800) 334-5551; http://www.carolina.com

**Connecticut Valley Biological
Supply Co., Inc.**
82 Valley Road, Box 326
Southampton, MA 01073
(800) 628-7748

Delta Education
P.O. Box 915
Hudson, NH 03051-0915
(800) 258-1302

Edmund Scientific Co.
101 East Gloucester Pike
Barrington, NJ 08007
(609) 547-3488

Educational Innovations, Inc.
151 River Road
Cos Cob, CT 06807-2514
http://www.teachersource.com

Fisher Science Education
485 S. Frontage Road
Burr Ridge, IL 60521
(800) 955-4663
http://www.fisheredu.com

Frey Scientific
100 Paragon Parkway
Mansfield, OH 44903
(800) 225-3739

Nasco-Fort Atkinson
P.O. Box 901
Fort Atkinson, WI 53538-0901
(800) 558-9595

Nasco-Modesto
P.O. Box 3837
Modesto, CA 95352-3837
(800) 558-9595
http://www.nascofa.com/prod/Home

Sargent-Welch/VWR Scientific
P.O. Box 5229
Buffalo Grove, IL 60089-5229
(800) SAR-GENT
http://www.SargentWelch.com

Science Kit & Boreal Laboratories
777 East Park Drive
Tonawanda, NY 14150
(800) 828-7777
http://sciencekit.com

Ward's Natural Science Establishment, Inc.
P.O. Box 92912
Rochester, NY 14692-9012
(800) 962-2660
http://www.wardsci.com

Toys mentioned in the text can sometimes be found at garage sales and flea markets, as well as in stores.

Further Reading

Books

Adams, Richard, and Robert Gardner. *Ideas for Science Projects, Revised edition.* Danbury, Conn.: Franklin Watts, 1997.

———. *More Ideas for Science Projects, Revised Edition.* Danbury, Conn.: Franklin Watts, 1998.

Bochinski, Julianne Blair. *The Complete Handbook of Science Fair Projects.* New York: John Wiley, 1996.

Friedhoffer, Robert. *Toying Around with Science: The Physics Behind Toys and Gags,* New York: Franklin Watts, 1995.

Gardner, Robert. *Experiments with Bubbles.* Springfield, N.J.: Enslow Publishers, Inc., 1995.

Gardner, Robert, and David Webster. *Experiments with Balloons.* Springfield, N.J.: Enslow Publishers, Inc., 1995.

Herbert, Don. *Mr. Wizard's Supermarket Science.* New York: Random House, 1980.

Krieger, Melanie Jacobs. *How to Excel in Science Competitions: Revised and Updated.* Springfield, N.J.: Enslow Publishers, Inc., 1999.

Newton, David E. *Making and Using Scientific Equipment.* New York: Franklin Watts, 1993.

Noddy, Tom. *Tom Noddy's Bubble Magic.* Philadelphia: Running Press, 1988.

Potter, Jean. *Science in Seconds with Toys: Over 100 Experiments You Can Do in Ten Minutes or Less.* New York: John Wiley, 1998.

Sneider, Cary I. *Experimenting with Model Rockets.* Berkeley, Calif.: Lawrence Science, 1991.

Stine, Megan. *Hands-On Science: Games, Puzzles, and Toys.* Milwaukee: Gareth Stevens, 1993.

Tocci, Salvatore. *How to Do a Science Fair Project. Revised edition.* Danbury, Conn.: Franklin Watts, 1997.

Wiese, Jim. *Roller Coaster Science: 50 Flying, Flipping, Spinning Gadgets Kids Create for Themselves.* New York: John Wiley, 1995.

Internet Addresses

Bloomfield, Louis A. *How Things Work.* n.d. <http://rabi. phys.virginia.edu/HTW>

The Exploratorium. *Exploratorium Home Page.* 1999. <http://www. exploratorium.edu/>

The Franklin Institute Science Museum. 1995–1999. <http://sln.fi. edu/>

International Racing and Rollercoaster Design Agency. n.d. <http:// dimacs.rutgers.edu/~dmollica/starttoys.html>

Morano, David. *Guide to Doing Science Fair Projects.* May 27, 1995. <http://www.isd77.k12.mn.us/resources/cf/SciProjIntro.html>

National Aeronautics and Space Administration. *Aerodynamics in Car Racing.* October 20, 1999. <http://www.nas.nasa.gov/ About/Education/Racecar/>

Index

A

air car, 22–24
    electric and magnetic forces
        on, 27–310
    forces on, 25–30
    as gravity detector, 24
astrolabe, 88–92

B

backspin, 74–75
balancing toy, 15–21
balloon in a bottle, 69–70
balloons, 63–70
    experiments with, 63–75
    and thermal expansion, 68
    as rocket launchers, 70
balls
    bounce height of different
        kinds, 71–72
    curved paths, 73–75
Bernoulli, Daniel, 66
    Ping-Pong ball and air
        pressure, 66
bounce, 71–72
brakes, 51–52
    on inclines, 51–52
bubbles, 117–120, 121

C

cars (toy) with springs, 56–59
    and exchange of energy,
        58–59
    collisions between, 56–59
cars and trucks (toys), 36–91
    effect of gravity, 45–46
    effect of height on distance,
        40–41
    effect of incline length on
        distance, 41–42
    effect of weight on
        distance, 41
    on "hills," 40–42
    safety and seat belts, 60–61
center of gravity, 15, 17, 21
centripetal force, 93, 95
clay boats, 115–116
    float or sink, 115–116
collisions, 56–59
comeback toy, 12–14
curve balls, 73–75

D

dipping or drinking bird, 110–111
    factors that affect drinking
        rate, 110–111

E

electric and magnetic forces,
    27–30
electric motor, 31, 33

F

first law of motion, 36, 95
Franklin, Benjamin, 64
    and definition of positive
        and negative charge, 64
friction, 22, 24, 25, 27

G

gears, 108–109
gravity, 45–46, 84, 93
    and centripetal force, 93
    and satellite orbits, 93

K

kinetic energy, 48, 59

L

loop-the-loop and toy cars, 48–50
 and electric cars, 49–50
 and gravitational potential
  energy, 48
 and kinetic energy, 48
 and spheres, 48

M

magnetic cars, 53–54
 collisions between, 53–54
magnetic force, 27, 28, 53–55
marbles, 43

P

Ping-Pong ball and air pressure,
 66
potential energy, 48, 59, 109
pressure, 112–113
 of air, 113
 as related to sled, skis,
  toboggan, and snow
  shoes on snow, 113
projectiles, 78–95
Push-N-Go®, 108–109
 and gears, 108–109
 and potential energy, 109
 effect of surface on travel
  distance, 108

R

ratio of circumference:diameter,
 100–101
rockets
 balloon, 87
 finding height of, 86–92
 launchers, 70

S

safety, 9–10
satellites, 93
 path in absence of gravity,
  93–95

science fairs, 8–9
seat belt, 60–61
second law of motion, 84
spheres on "hills," 43–44
spinning top toy, 36–37
static electricity and balloons,
 64–65
Superball, 71

T

telephone toy, 34
temperature and expansion of a
 gas, 68
thickness of soap bubbles,
 117–120
third law of motion, 86, 87
topspin, 74–75

W

wagons and forces, 103–105
 effects of force on speed,
  103–104
 effects of weight on
  friction, 104
wagons and wheels, 98–101
 and axles, 98
 to measure distance,
  99–100
 path of bug on wheel's rim,
  100
walking toys
 speed of, 106–107
water "bombs," 84–85
 dropping from a bicycle, 85
water guns, 78–83
 and firing angle, 81–82
 and pressurized air, 80
 range, 80–81
water projectiles, 78–83
 speed of, 78–79
 time of flight, 79–80

Harris County Public Library
Houston, Texas